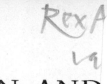

D1485787

MAN AND

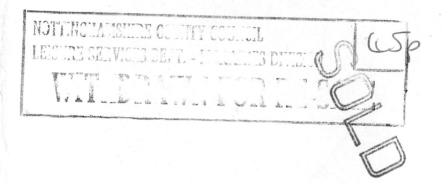

MAN
AND NATURE

edited by
HUGH MONTEFIORE

with a foreword by
the Right Reverend Michael Ramsey

Q. contributor (P. Oestreicher)

COLLINS
St James's Place, London
1975

William Collins Sons & Co Ltd
London · Glasgow · Sydney · Auckland
Toronto · Johannesburg

First published 1975
ISBN 0 00 215524 9
Set in Monotype Bembo
Made and Printed in Great Britain by
William Collins Sons & Co Ltd Glasgow

CONTENTS

FOREWORD

by the Right Revd Lord Ramsey of Canterbury

Amidst much practical concern and action about the 'environment', and much exhortation on behalf of such concern and action, there has been the need for a presentation of the Christian understanding of the matter. What are the implications of Christian belief for man's attitude to the environment in which he lives? This book explores the answer. It draws upon the traditions of Christian teaching about man's relation to the world, and it interprets that tradition with the aid of contemporary knowledge. I believe that it meets a need, and fills a serious gap.

I think that this book will be valued within ecumenical circles as an Anglican contribution to contemporary discussion. Anglicans have long cherished a theology which has strongly emphasized the Incarnation. Incarnational theology has had its limitations, but this book shows how its exponents by drawing out things both old and new can speak to an urgent contemporary situation.

I am glad and proud to have had a small share in encouraging the writing of this book, which was completed a few weeks before I retired from office. It will have many grateful readers who will be stirred to a new concern about the Christian attitude to the world of which we human beings are a part.

† Michael Ramsey

MAN AND NATURE
THE WORKING GROUP

A small group was appointed by the Archbishop of Canterbury in 1971 to work in connection with the Doctrine Commission of the Church of England, with the following terms of reference: 'To investigate the relevance of Christian doctrine to the problems of man in his environment.' The group began its work on 25 February 1972. Ten meetings were held, seven of which were residential; and this report was presented to Dr Michael Ramsey in October 1974, shortly before his retirement. The following were appointed members of the group:

*Hugh Montefiore	*Chairman:* Bishop Suffragan of Kingston-upon-Thames
*A. M. Allchin	Canon Residentiary of Canterbury Cathedral
Don Cupitt	Fellow and Dean of Emmanuel College, Cambridge; Lecturer in Divinity, Cambridge University
Mary Hesse	Fellow of Wolfson College, Cambridge; Professor of the Philosophy of Science, Cambridge University
*John Macquarrie	Canon of Christ Church, Oxford; Lady Margaret Professor of Divinity, Oxford
*A. R. Peacocke	Fellow and Dean of Clare College, Cambridge

* Member of the Doctrine Commission of the Church of England.

Canon Michael Green had to resign from the group at an early stage due to pressure of work. The group owes a debt of gratitude to the Revd Ian Duffield, who acted throughout as secretarial assistant.

While the report was still at a draft stage the group was helped by a lengthy discussion with the Doctrine Commission. The report, which has been kept comparatively short, has been augmented by essays by individual authors spelling out important aspects of the subject in greater depth than would be appropriate within the confines of the report itself. The group is particularly grateful to Canon John Austin Baker and the Revd Paul Oestreicher, who were not members of the group, but who have contributed valuable essays in fields beyond the expertise of any of its members.

The group acknowledges with gratitude assistance received from the following by correspondence, memoranda or papers: Canon John Austin Baker, the Revd Professor John Bowker, Mrs Mary Z. Brittain, Mr Derek Bryan, the Rt Revd Dr Kenneth Cragg, Professor Anthony Hewish, FRS, the Revd Kenneth Leech, the Revd Professor E. L. Mascall, Dr Joseph Needham, FRS, the Revd Paul Oestreicher, the Revd Professor Norman Pittenger, Professor Ninian Smart, the Revd Professor T. F. Torrance, Professor Lynn White, and Professor Monica Wilson.

The group also acknowledges the initial stimulus received from a meeting in 1971 of Dr Norman Moore and Dr Max Nicholson with the Doctrine Commission, which led to the request by the late Dr I. T. Ramsey, then chairman of the Commission, that this group be set up.

MAN AND NATURE
THE REPORT

I
INTRODUCTION:
THE WORLD WE LIVE IN

Progress or Collapse?

Twentieth-century civilization is proving remarkably turbulent and crisis-ridden. At the beginning of the century Europe was at the centre of the stage, and it was from a ferocious clash of European nationalisms that the United States and the Soviet Union emerged as the countries of the future. The First World War accelerated the pace of technical development, mass-production and mass-communication, leading to economic collapse, and, in some countries, political totalitarianism. A second, even more disastrous, war inaugurated the atomic era. Yet beneath that shadow new technical and economic skills were able to create a generation of prosperity and expansion. The rich countries relegated wars to the margins of the developed world. But fresh sources of anxiety appeared as the dangers became successively apparent, of over-population in the mid-fifties, of pollution in the late fifties, and of resource-exhaustion in the sixties.

By 1970 matters were coming to a head. The richer countries were becoming over-extended: most of them were becoming over-populated, over-industrialized, and over-reliant upon cheap imported raw materials, while (in the new situation of nuclear stalemate) they could no longer secure either their supplies or their markets by the threat of military force. Meanwhile resources were either becoming less plentiful or were being deliberately withheld by the producing countries in the interests of long-term conservation, and of extracting a full market-price. World commodity prices and energy costs began to rise very steeply, and chronic world-wide inflation set in, causing political instability within and between nations. What the outcome will be is anybody's guess. Men are very adaptable and inventive; but there is an uncomfortable gap between the high rate of political change and the slow rate (or 'lead time') at which, for example, new energy sources can be developed on the vast scale required. So the outlook is very uncertain.

The twentieth century has seen the most rapid technical development in human history. People born before powered flight saw men walk on the moon. Within five decades medicine moved from leeches and cupping to organ transplants. We are seeing the most rapid population-growth, and we have seen the greatest wars in history. Whole nations have passed from preliterate tribal culture to modern statehood in a generation.

There are great reserves of adaptability, not only in man himself, but in natural ecosystems. But there are limits. We have to ask the question, what is the relation of man to his own nature, and to external nature? Can the natural world and man's own nature stand the strains to which both are now being subjected? What are we doing, to the world and to ourselves?

In the book of Genesis God tells man to fill and rule the earth, a command which long sustained men in the hard struggle between themselves and wild nature. But in the present century the relation of man to nature has changed rapidly. Men's numbers, and the rate at which they are transforming the environment and consuming resources and energy, have

suddenly leapt upwards. This is happening at different rates in
different countries. Seeing it from the air, one is reminded that
the English landscape has been almost entirely man-made for a
long time, whereas Siberia is only just beginning to be domesticated. But, in general, much of the world is now being
developed very rapidly, including even the sea, for so many
centuries the symbol of primal chaos and untameable natural
force. The sea-bed is being opened for exploitation, and the
chemistry of the sea, the movements of its waters, and the
numbers and distribution of living things within it are being
monitored now with a view to being managed in the future.

This qualitative change in the human situation arouses mixed
feelings of exhilaration and alarm. To some it seems that we
are humanizing the world, building the New Jerusalem, and so
fulfilling the aims of religion and socialism alike. There may
be difficulties along the way, but they are soluble. But to others
it seems that the hope of our filling and ruling the earth is
turning sour as it is realized, and the prospect ahead seems
nightmarish.

Another effect of the new human situation is this: as our
environment, and the forces which shape our lives, become
more and more man-made, our basic thoughts about ourselves
and our situation become more and more anthropocentric.
Pre-industrial man was up against a rich and meaningful
non-human reality. Through ritual and poetry he sought to
manage and place himself in relation to animals, the soil, the
weather, spirits, fortune and death. His sense of who he was
depended upon the symbolic *rapport* he created between
himself and the non-human. But modern urban man lives in
an inanimate man-made environment, which reflects back to
him only his own uncertain image.

Perhaps the greatest problem we face is that of our own

numbers. The population issue exemplifies the curious 'blindness' of modern developments, for we are far from understanding why the population explosion has occurred or how to control it.[1] Fertility remains a mystery, and it is not easy to demonstrate any very substantial result of the efforts of governments either to increase population-growth (as in Eastern Europe) or to limit it (as in India). Nor do we fully understand why many peoples (as in the Amazon basin) have lost their fertility and simply died out. In some areas of life our powers are so great that modern man has been compared with a god, but in other areas we are reminded of how little understanding and control he yet has over the forces that rule him.

More people need more food: but food-supply remains problematic. We know little of how population was controlled in the earliest times. Man has always been a wanderer, and maybe early men simply moved on when their numbers became too great: possibly that is why man has long been more widely distributed than any other vertebrate. But in any case that solution is no longer possible. The world now depends heavily upon North American surpluses, and North America still has agricultural capacity in reserve. But North American agriculture is highly energy-intensive; that is to say, its ability to save us from famine depends upon the maintenance of the same technical-industrial society whose instability is at the root of our problems. It is not easy to see how man can get into a controlled relationship (one that is *not* incipiently catastrophic) with his environment. Although China and a few African states claim to see the need for equilibrium, it is ominous that newly rich countries like Persia and Brazil plan to develop at a far more ruthless pace than Europe or the USA ever attempted.

Underlying Assumptions

The modern world is governed by beliefs and historical forces which originated mainly in Europe. Indeed, many of them began in Britain as much as anywhere else. Democratic forms of government in place of absolute monarchy, the scientific revolution, the industrial revolution, the population explosion, mass-emigration and the colonization of underpopulated territories, the development of mechanized transport, mass-production and mass-communication – in all these areas Britain, to a greater or lesser extent, was in the van.

By now people have come to think of Europe as typically activist and aggressive, but it was not always so. Much of the older religious and metaphysical thought of Europe was as other-worldly and contemplative in its emphasis as Indian thought. In the traditions of Plato and Christian monasticism the Supreme Good for man was seen in terms of reason, theory and contemplation rather than will, practice and technical manipulation. Social thought was set against the background of a stable cosmic order governed by transcendent norms, rather than seen in terms of an onrushing historical process subject to the human will.

But there was also a 'natural magic' or hermetic tradition which sees man as a *magus* (like Faust, or Doctor Who in the television programme) who penetrates forbidden mysteries, acquires hidden knowledge, and so gains power, divine power, over nature by understanding her secret workings. Historians nowadays stress the importance of this tradition in the development, first of Renaissance humanism, and then of early modern science.

At any rate, the shift of emphasis took place, from God to man; from heaven to earth; from ritual and symbolism to observation and mathematical analysis; and from a timeless sacral order to an ongoing historical process. Hobbes (*Leviathan*, 1651) illustrates the change when he says that motion, not rest, is fundamental. There is no *summum bonum*, or Perfect Good, because human existence is nothing but an insatiable and endless striving after power. From Leibniz (*c.* 1700) onwards the idea of progress becomes more and more important. Saint-Simon (*c.* 1800) linked it with the industrial revolution, and Marx and Engels first assert plainly that the character of any society is determined more than anything else by the nature and ownership of its means of production. Man is *homo faber*, man the worker, whose business is to transform and humanize nature by his work.

Yet even in Saint-Simon and Marx science and technology are still means, rather than ends. They are still subordinate to an ethical and humanistic vision of the goals of life. We tend, in retrospect, to exaggerate the importance of science before the present century. Even by 1900 there were still only two thousand science graduates in Britain, of whom only one-eighth were employed in industry.[2]

But somewhere in the second half of the nineteenth century the modern ideology took shape, perhaps in the generation of Ernest Renan,[3] perhaps in that of Edison and H. G. Wells. People began to think that science is far and away the principal agent of social change, and will determine the future of man. Religion, morality and philosophy no longer matter very much, because they do not effectively determine the goals of life. The real power belongs to a process of scientific discovery, technical innovation, industrial application and economic growth – the whole leading to ever greater prosperity and well-being.

So in our century the science-based industrial system has become a gigantic social force, 'development' as it is called. Like the population explosion, like 'capital', its dynamic movement is no longer clearly under human control, nor subordinated to a vision of the purposes which are to be achieved by it. So far as it has any philosophical presuppositions they may be called broadly utilitarian. Men at large seek pleasure, comfort and security, and shun pain, discomfort and insecurity. Government's job is to manage the economy and stimulate technology so as to attain these goods and distribute them widely. When the 'standard of living' is rising rapidly the government is strong; when it is static or falling the government is weak. Any wider vision is liable to be ridiculed as 'ideology' or 'idealism'. A broadly Benthamite model of man, egoistic and acquisitive, has come to be presupposed in the key areas of national life, and a kind of systematic blindness to the question of ends has developed. Yet for the mass of men the benefits of the new order are indisputable, and only recently attained. In Britain itself, the oldest industrial country, it is only since the Second World War that the mass of working-class children have reached a decent standard of diet, clothing, housing, health and education, and even yet there is scarcely room for complacency. It is not surprising that people are fiercely attached to an order of things which has only so recently begun to deliver such substantial and undeniable benefits.

Technology

Nor do tradition or religion give us any reason to disparage technology. Jew, Christian and Moslem all saw creation from the first in technical rather than biological terms. God makes the world like a craftsman, rather than begets it like a parent. Our religious traditions always saw something divine in the exercise of a craft, and spoke of God as a potter, a master-builder, a furnaceman or a husbandman.[4]

And every human society has a technology, in the sense of organized methods of appropriating and using the resources of nature to obtain food, heal the sick, and build tools, weapons, boats and houses. Every society's technology is shaped by and in turn shapes its forms of social life and its world-picture. Religious change, social change and technical change all run together, influencing each other; and disorder in one realm reflects and exacerbates disorder in the others.

For example, in the seventeenth century men became more and more fascinated with machines. Eventually mechanistic patterns of thinking prevailed in natural philosophy. The world itself is a great machine, animal bodies are machines, the human body is a machine, man himself is perhaps 'nothing but' a machine. Hence began a fascination with automata, robots and computers which has lasted to the present day. The machine, something man has made himself, becomes the thing over against himself through which man seeks to understand himself. Machine analogies begin to get out of hand when politics becomes social engineering, the cure of souls becomes behaviour technology, architecture becomes the provision of machines for living in, and even education is done by teaching machines. People begin to feel uneasy about the extent to which life begins to be dominated by mechanistic ways of thinking.

But the moral of this is not that we can and should create a society with no technology. It is rather that technology, as a thing of great power, can as well be used for evil ends as good; and where there is not enough thought about ends it will tend to be used, in the long run, for evil ends; for that is the way the world in general, and human nature in particular, are constituted.

The Ends of Action

For a generation or more the presumption has been that politicians will get votes, and social harmony will be maintained, so long as the masses can be provided with an ever-improving material standard of living. But now ever-rising expectations are running up against fast-approaching physical limits; so where do we turn? Religion, art, and moral and political confidence have languished, and are not at present in any condition to provide alternative forms of satisfaction on the vast scale required. We face the danger of acute disillusionment and political instability, because our method of development has raised people's expectations too high, and often in the wrong directions.

To say this is to invite a bitter retort from some modern Marxists. They will say that, having discovered our mistake in drugging the masses with commodities as a substitute for a truly human life, we are now thinking that it would be prudent to revert to older opiates. There is some justice in this criticism. But the problems of today transcend the ideological conflict between capitalism and socialism. Socialist countries are not exempt from the possibility of a disorderly and unstable relation of man to nature. They too may encounter over-population, and have experienced food shortages, over-industrialization, over-reliance on fossil fuels, and the decay of work-satisfaction, human relationships, and art, which accompanies mass-production in factories. The crisis is hitting capitalist countries first because they are more 'developed' rather than because they are capitalist; and socialist countries are eager to 'develop' too. And there are reasons for thinking that the troubles of the twentieth century have to do with a kind of extreme anthropocentrism, and a purely instrumental view of nature, to which socialism has usually been strongly committed.

For it is the extreme anthropocentrism of modern culture which makes many of its problems so intractable. In the seventeenth century ideas of purpose and value were expelled from natural philosophy by men like Galileo and Descartes. The long-term result has been a concentration of religious meaning, of artistic and moral value, and of ideas of purpose within man himself. The external world is without intrinsic value or meaning. It exists only as raw material for man's use. There is nothing external to man which has moral authority over him; which has a right to constrain him, or to check his ambition. Thus there is no way of describing a moral equilibrium between man and his environment.

Animals illustrate the problem, for, as everyone knows, various animals are in danger of becoming extinct in the wild state. They compete with man, for example, because they stand at the heads of food-chains (like the great aquatic mammals), or because their way of life is such that they need large areas of forest to roam in undisturbed (like the great apes). Apes, elephants, whales and many other creatures cost, or will soon cost, human lives to preserve. But if man himself is the measure of all things and the only source of value, how can there be rational arbitration between men and orang-utans? Science describes such creatures, but it does not evaluate them. Economists may set an economic value upon a game reserve, but that is value to and for man; and our question is not about their value to man, but about the *intrinsic* value of elephants, apes and, for that matter, even the malaria parasite.

So the question we put to Marxists and other thorough-going humanists is this: while our ethic and our world-view are so anthropocentric, how can man and nature ever get into balance? We believe that what is needed is a religious world-picture which portrays a common order under which man and his fellow-creatures live, and which gives a framework within which we can relate man, his work, and organic and inorganic nature to each other.

This objective created order, if we can define it, will be a middle way between nature as demonic (primitive culture) and nature as purely instrumental to human purposes (modern anthropocentrism). And it would provide a context (the macrocosm) in which man can grasp what is his own nature (as microcosm). So for us it is the true humanism. Autonomous and man-centred humanism is, in truth, in some difficulty over the concept of human nature. Many Marxists and existentialists deny that there is any constant objectively determined human nature; and yet at the same time propose to educe all ideas of value from man himself, look to the 'humanization' of nature, and seek 'a truly human life' as their ideal. But how can human nature be malleable and subject to endless future transformation, and at the same time be the sole source of norms? How can degrees either of alienation or of progress be measured without any norms external to man by which to measure them?

In fact we are searching, at this point, for a doctrine of creation; or, more broadly, a theology of nature. For when the world is seen as creation, it is seen as being analogous to a work of art. This has two obvious consequences: first, the diversity of creatures is seen as valuable; and secondly, all the creatures comprise an evolving, interdependent created order, in which everything is connected to everything else. Things are valuable both in themselves, and as parts of the whole order.[5]

When we said that a particular species of animal should be regarded as *intrinsically* valuable, we did not mean that its value is *absolute*. Again, the best analogy is with a work of art. We may regard a work of art as intrinsically valuable, but nevertheless agree that the Government is right when it refuses to release a convicted terrorist in order to save a work of art from the threat of destruction. Similarly, it may be that a particular weed-killer ought still to be introduced, even though a side-effect will be the extinction of a particular species of butterfly. But at least, if the butterfly species is regarded as intrinsically valuable, it will be given some real weight in the calculations which precede the introduction of the weed-killer. In both cases, the choice is between two goods, not between a real benefit and something of merely sentimental interest. Of course it is true that in a changing world not all good things can be preserved; but neither need we continue on a course of unthinking destruction.

To see the world as creation involves a very large-scale change in our overall attitude to the world we live in, and our operations in it. When we describe the new perspective, it seems platitudinous; but when the platitude is taken seriously, it has immense consequences. In the nineteenth century a few people suddenly started taking seriously the platitude that women are free, rational, moral agents just as men are – with social implications which will go on reverberating for a long time yet. Similarly, to take the idea of creation seriously will be to initiate immense changes.

There are of course different views of the world as creation, even within the Christian tradition – differences which we have discovered among ourselves, and which are reflected in what follows. For it is to the Christian idea of creation that we now turn.

2

THE GOD WHO CREATES

The Idea of Creation

'Why is there something rather than nothing?' The question arises when men step aside from the business of living to reflect upon the world, and find in themselves a sense of wonder at their own existence and that of the world. Awareness of death is part of what it means to be human, and this brings the realization that there is nothing necessary about our existence. It is contingent; it might not *be* at all. Then we become aware of the contingent character of the things that surround us, and we pass even to wondering about the contingent character of the universe itself. Moreover, in face of much apparent chaos and frustration in the world, we want to be able to see that the universe 'makes sense'. We need what Geoffrey Moorhouse has called 'our focal point and our security', without which 'we are people spinning helplessly and hopelessly through a fearful void'.[1]

In spite of the ban positivist philosophers tried to impose upon such metaphysical and seemingly unanswerable questions, recent philosophy has become more adventurous. For example, in a detailed analysis of the traditional question about there being something rather than nothing, Milton K. Munitz has contended that the question is better formulated: 'Is there a reason for the world's existence?' He argues that this is a perfectly meaningful question, even though we can give no scientific answer to it.[2]

The Christian seeks to answer the question 'Is there a reason for the world's existence?' by the doctrine of creation. This is not a scientific answer arrived at by processes of inquiry such as we might employ to answer the question 'Is there a reason for the rise and fall of the tides?' It is an answer that stems from the mythico-religious realm of thought. Behind the doctrine of creation stands the *myth* of creation. 'Myth' is not used here in the sense of a fictitious story that deliberately falsifies science and history, but rather of a story that interprets whatever the facts are that constitute science and history. Discovery of the facts is undoubtedly important, but in addition men have always told stories expressing their sense of wonder and their need to see meaning in the facts. A myth should not be so interpreted as blatantly to contradict what is known, but it should provide a framework of significance in terms of which sense can be made of the world. Not all frameworks are equally good. We can compare frameworks by asking which fit more facts into a coherent whole, and which take into account and allow better for earlier meanings that have been found authentic in human experience.[3]

The classical Judeo-Christian story is reduced to its briefest form in the opening verse of the Bible: 'In the beginning God created the heavens and the earth' (Genesis 1:1). Every expression in this verse calls for comment.[4]

'In the beginning . . .' This expression is typical of a myth. It might seem that we are dealing here with mythical or archetypal time, not with historical or datable time as we now understand it. But there is an important difference between the primal myths of the Old Testament and those of other ancient Near Eastern peoples. The latter belong to a 'timeless' world, but the Old Testament myths are linked to the historical process through the device of the genealogy. The Old Testament creation story is to be understood therefore as a mythical account of the beginning of history.

'God.' The use of God-language makes it clear that this is not a scientific explanation of the world, nor a 'hypothesis' in the scientific sense. God-language belongs, in Paul van Buren's expression, to 'the edges of language'.[5] The word 'God' in Judeo-Christian usage also implies a reality which includes personality and rationality. So in using this language, we are claiming that the ultimate reason for the world's existence is not less than personal and rational. This is certainly a meaningful assertion, for we can see how it contradicts other meaningful assertions, for instance Jacques Monod's view that the universe exists purely by chance.[6] Here are two conflicting answers to the question about the world, both meaningful, and both claiming to be true. It is important that we should be able to point in this way to an alternative answer, for this indicates that the answer in terms of God is certainly not vacuous.

'. . . created.' It is surely very remarkable that Hebrew, a language with a rather limited vocabulary, does not use the common verb *asa* ('made'), but a quite special verb, *bara* ('created'). It is not known exactly what this verb meant originally, but in the Hebrew scriptures it is used only with God as subject. The use of this special verb is highly important, for it stresses that 'creation' by God is thought of as a unique relationship. It may be *analogous to* but cannot be identified with 'making', and this is a point to which we shall return when we come to discuss models of creation. Incidentally, the choice of *bara* rather than *asa* does *not* appear to have anything to do with the notion of 'creation out of nothing', which is not part of the Genesis story.

18

'. . . the heavens and the earth.' This is the Hebrew phrase for what we would now call the 'universe' or 'world'. We can only describe the universe to the extent that we know about it, and of course the heavens and the earth known to the Hebrews formed a much more compact world than the universe as we know it today. The creation story therefore needs to be set continually against man's expanding knowledge of the world.

Although the story did not emerge as a scientific answer to the question about the existence of the world, rational considerations are not irrelevant. It is conceivable that increasing empirical understanding of the universe might seem to count against a particular expression of the doctrine of creation; for example, the idea that the explanation for the existence of the world is to be found in a reality not less than personal and rational. Two examples of expanding scientific knowledge might be given as counting against this creation doctrine. The first is Monod's view that the evolution of man has come about purely by chance, and the other concerns the second law of thermodynamics.

Monod's arguments will be examined in more detail in the essay 'On the Alleged Incompatibility between Christianity and Science'. There it is maintained that even within the context of biological theory the arguments do not show that only chance has been operative, for there must at least be an initial structure in matter upon which chance and its laws can operate – a *potentiality* for matter to develop the forms of organic molecules and living species that we know to exist. This potentiality can be no more than an arbitrary given from the point of view of science, a datum whose occurrence is explained neither by laws nor by chance. But beyond this, even if Monod had been correct in concluding that evolution is only a process of chance trial and error, excluding the possibility of purposive design, he would still not have disproved the creation of the world by God. It may be that God, like ourselves, experiments to try out all the potentialities of his creation and runs through many possible combinations and arrangements. Perhaps we are inclined to expect too much in the way of systematic purpose in every aspect of the creation. Surely God too can play, and can create the beautiful for its own sake?[7]

The other example concerns the second law of thermo-dynamics. Perhaps the universe is gradually running down and will end up motionless and dead. Would this falsify the doctrine of creation? In the first place we have to note that it is now acknowledged as quite uncertain whether the entropy increase which affects any closed system applies to the universe as a whole, for the universe may not be a closed system. But even if universal death is to be its fate, this would still not in itself disprove the creation doctrine, for the history of the uni-verse might have timeless worth. To believe in a creator God is to believe that the physical universe is not the whole of reality.

It is difficult to find scientific hypotheses which could con-clusively refute the doctrine of creation. The relation between creation stories and science is too complex for that. Philosophers of science now recognize that even scientific hypotheses are related to their data in a more complex way than simple em-pirical falsifiability. But developing scientific knowledge may affect the way in which a doctrine of creation is interpreted or presented, as has happened many times since the Genesis story was written. For example, it was generally believed until the nineteenth century that the story committed Christians to belief in a creation at a datable time at a few millennia BC.[8] But the story is compatible with many different scientific hypotheses, and is also susceptible of interpretation in terms of many different models of the creator-world relation.

Models of Creation

Can we say more clearly what is meant by this word 'create'? We have seen that in the Bible a special word was used to denote a unique relation, the relation between God and the world. We have seen further that this relation is not confined to any single period or point of time, such as a putative beginning of the history of the universe. It expresses the constant relation subsisting between God and the world, whereby he maintains the world in being.

We can also say that this is an asymmetrical relation. It is a relation in which the world is derived from and depends upon him. The contingent character of worldly being is traced back to God, who is not contingent.

The mode of being of God is therefore essentially different from the mode of being of the created world. But in order to describe God at all and his relation to the world, we are bound to make use of analogies from ordinary human models of creation. In seeking models for God and his actions, it is therefore of the utmost importance to employ more than one model. No model or analogy can contain God or represent him without distortion. No single model should be given a monopoly, otherwise it almost inevitably ceases to be understood analogically and is understood literally, with the result that its particular distortion is absolutized. If there are several models, one helps to correct the other. We may compare the situation to the attempt to represent the surface of the earth on a flat

surface. This cannot be done without distortion. Some projections distort areas, while others represent areas correctly
but distort shapes. We use different projections for different
purposes, and we are not misled, because one projection cor-
rects another. But in principle there could never be a projection
that would represent a curved surface on a flat surface without
distortion.

In different religions, and even in different forms of Christian
theology, sometimes models of the transcendence of God over
the world have been stressed, sometimes those of his immanence
in the world. What would be incompatible with Christianity
would be a doctrine either of the total immanence of God
(pantheism, which tends to identify God and the world), or of
his total transcendence (deism, in the sense of the doctrine of a
distant God who has no effective interaction with the world).
But although these two positions are strictly incompatible
with Christian faith, theologians have in fact at various times
moved close to them.

Models stressing the transcendence of God have been overwhelmingly dominant in the history of theology. The model
of creation as a 'making' has been almost absolutized in Christian
tradition, and has tended to exclude others and to emphasize
its own kind of distortion. Closely allied to it is the monarchical
model, derived from biblical sources, which dominated theology
in the sixteenth and seventeenth centuries, when the age of
absolute monarchy in Europe coincided with the formative
period of modern theology in the Reformation and Counter-
Reformation. Calvin's stress on the sovereignty of God and
likewise some of the language in the Book of Common Prayer
('high and mighty, King of kings, Lord of lords, the only Ruler
of princes, who dost from thy throne behold all the dwellers
upon earth . . .') go far toward justifying William James' quip

that God was conceived as a kind of Louis XIV of the heavens. Yet the emergence of deism makes it clear that a God so highly exalted is in danger of losing touch with his people and becoming finally a distant peripheral figure.

The model of 'making' is already used in the biblical narrative. God 'made' the firmament, the lights in the sky, and he said, 'Let us make man.' In each case the common Hebrew verb *asa* is used. An analogy is being established between God's creative acts and human acts of making. Theologians have often maintained that this analogy finally breaks down because God makes the creatures out of nothing, whereas all human making works with an already existing material. But the real problem about the adequacy of the model of making is different. It has often been claimed that something which is made is entirely external to the maker and a product of his will, and it has therefore been argued that the creation is entirely external to God. It was by a free and sovereign act of will that the creation was brought into existence, and it is usually implied that God might equally well have refrained from creating. Indeed, herein lies the contingency of the creation. This view received classic statement from Calvin and more recently in those writings of Barth and Brunner in which the difference and distance between Creator and creation are stressed to the limit.

The most recent advocates of this view are the so-called 'theologians of the secular', both Protestant and Catholic, such as F. Gogarten,[9] Harvey Cox[10] and J. Metz.[11] They have been insistent in declaring that the world is quite external to God and is therefore stripped of any numinous quality, and so available to man's exploitation. According to Cox, the Hebrew understanding of creation 'separates nature from God'. Nature has become 'disenchanted': 'This disenchantment of the natural world provides an absolute precondition for the development of natural science' and 'makes nature itself available for man's use'.[12]

It was first argued by Max Weber, in *The Protestant Ethic and the Spirit of Capitalism* (1905), and subsequently by Robert Merton[13] and others, that the Calvinist tradition of various Protestant Churches and sects brought about a changed attitude to the natural world that helped to form not only the economic system of capitalism, but also the new science and ultimately the technological exploitation of 'disenchanted' nature. Some modern secular writers, such as Herbert Marcuse[14] and Theodore Roszak,[15] have attacked the Calvinist legacy detected by Weber precisely on the grounds that the scientific-technological tradition has depersonalized man and ravaged nature. Christian theology, however, has always exhibited two attitudes in tension with one another: the freedom of man to use nature on the one hand, and the sacramental character of nature as God's gift on the other. A divergence between Luther and Calvin illustrates this tension. Calvin stressed that the creation is not God, and his immediate disciples and successors perhaps exaggerated and over-simplified this into a dichotomy which leaves nature godless, and seems to free man from any inhibitions towards it. Luther, by contrast, insisted that the creation is *God's* creation and is therefore worthy of respect because it is the divine handiwork, and everything in it is therefore worthy to be an object of investigation by the human mind – even, to use his own example, 'the guts of a louse'. If one stresses with some followers of Calvin the separateness of nature from God and its essential godlessness, then the way is open to reckless and irresponsible exploitation. But if one stresses with Luther that this is God's creation and worthy of respect, investigation and use are certainly not inhibited, but these are likely to proceed in a more responsible way.

Accounts of the creation-relation which stress God's immanence have made use of models of organism and emanation.
That the world is related to God in some such way as the
interdependent parts of an organism, or as breath from the
body, suggests that the God-world relation is not entirely
asymmetrical, as in the monarchical model, but is in at least
some respects symmetrical. God puts himself into his creation,
is affected by it, and even to some extent vulnerable to it. The
creation is not totally external to God. Such doctrines certainly
offend against traditional ideas of the immutability and im-
passibility of God, and have therefore frequently been thought
heretical. But they do seem highly compatible both with the
belief in a loving God and with the belief in incarnation. They
deserve to be used as alternative models to counter extreme
monarchical or 'making' views, although they do not have the
same priority as the models of transcendence, which are
dominant in the Bible and in Christian tradition.

Some recent writers, such as Charles Hartshorne[16] and John
Robinson,[17] have revived the term 'panentheism' to denote a
doctrine which attempts to do justice to both transcendence
and immanence. This is not quite the pantheistic doctrine that
the world and God are identical, but rather that God *includes*
the world, that every part is 'in' him, but that he is not ex-
hausted by the world. In this school of thought, known as
'process theology', God is seen as so deeply involved in the
cosmic evolutionary process as almost to be identified with it,
at least in his concrete nature. Some of the American writers
to whom Robinson appeals come near to interpreting this as a
pure immanentism, though Robinson himself carefully avoids
this extreme position. In these American views, as Eric Mascall
puts it, the immanent God seems to evoke not so much adoration as sympathy.[18] Perhaps it is better not to try to unify the

different models too neatly in a single doctrine such as panen-theism, but to allow them to stand together and qualify one another in our thinking about God and the world. Two con-ditions seem to be required before we can properly use God-language. There must be a sense in which God is above the chances and changes of the world, yet there must also be a sense in which he is among them with us: to be God, he must be characterized by both power and love.

Another model of the God-world relation having much to commend it is that of an artist in relation to his work, for example, a painting. We do in fact use the word 'creative' about artists. The artist's work is certainly something which he 'makes', and in making it he transcends it. It is also external to himself. Yet at the same time the artist puts himself into his work, and there is a sense in which it is not merely external to him. It can be considered almost as an extension of the artist, a kind of 'emanation'.

Another image depicts the creation as a garment (Psalm 104:2). This is scarcely a prominent thought in the Bible, but it does suggest rather well both the distinctness of the creation from God, and yet the intimacy of the relation between God and his creation. One's clothes are not a part of one's body, yet they belong to one in a very intimate way, and to some extent express who one is.

More akin to the model of emanation is the biblical image of the creator Spirit 'moving over the face of the waters' (Genesis 1:2), or being breathed into man (Genesis 2:7; cf. also Psalm 104:30). John V. Taylor comments: 'To envisage creation in the image of life-giving energy is a far profounder insight than the image of God as potter or builder who remains outside and essentially separate from his handiwork.'[19]

A further image found in the Bible is that of Wisdom,

hypostatized as God's agent in creation (Proverbs 8:30). Connected with this is the image of the Word. With probable origins in Greek philosophy and Hellenistic thought as well as the Hebrew scriptures and Rabbinic speculation, the Word is akin to the model of emanation: it is both the Creator's internal power of creative reason and his outgoing creative power (John 1:1-3). In the New Testament the Word is used to interpret the nature of Jesus and so links together God's work of creation and salvation.

The way we combine these aspects of God's creative activity has important consequences for the value we set on creation and so for our practical attitudes. If creation is represented as resulting from an almost arbitrary act of will, so that it is a matter of indifference to God whether he creates or refrains from creating, then inevitably the created order is depreciated and deprived of intrinsic value. (This was the criticism of the biblical doctrine of creation propounded by Feuerbach.[20]) It would be equally mistaken to think that God necessarily creates the world. But if we see creation as proceeding from the loving being of God, and think that creating and sustaining others than himself are actions which accord with and express God's own personal being, this does confer value on the creation and promotes attitudes of caring and responsibility towards it.

Man and Creation

When we ask about man's relation to the creation we come again to the kinds of tension that have characterized the God-world relation. There we found it necessary to hold together the models of making and emanation, or monarchy and organic unity, though allowing a definite priority to those that

stress the 'otherness' of God. In the case of man, the tensions
and dualities are manifold. He is limited and he is free; he is
irrational and he is rational; he is animal and he is personal;
he is body and he is soul; he is individual and he is social – and
so the list goes on, a catalogue of apparently conflicting characteristics. In short, man is both creaturely and creative. This
contrast is essential to the Christian doctrine of man.

Man is a creature, part of that whole created realm which
God has brought forth. Man is bound to the rest of creation in
innumerable ways. His life is dependent on an environment
which must maintain itself within a fairly narrow range of
temperature and pressure. That environment must also make
available a constant supply of oxygen, water, and all the other
substances necessary for the support of life. From one point of
view, man is a physico-chemical system. He has arisen out of
the natural world and he continues to be part of it. He is dust,
indeed; but dust that has been built up into such intricate
patterns and that exhibits such incredibly complex dynamic
processes that, to a greater extent than any other creature known
to us, man has brought to light the undreamed of potentialities
of the natural world. The creature man also has affinity with
the other animals. He can be assigned a place in the animal
kingdom and he lives in terms of symbiosis and even a kind of
friendship with his domestic animals. We know that man,
animals, plants and even bacteria are all built up by the same
genetic materials. The interdependence of all living things is
stressed nowadays, in contrast to the stress that was laid on
struggle and competition in the nineteenth century. J. Z.
Young writes: 'All of us, animals, plants, and bacteria, form
one closely interlocked network of ecological relationships . . .
It is easy to elevate these facts into a pretentious scheme of the
whole living world as one "organism". Yet there is a sense in

28

which this is true. It is difficult to exaggerate our interdependence.'[21]

Thus, on one entire side of his being, man is a creature, inextricably involved with other creatures. He is and is likely to remain subject in many ways to the laws that hold in the physical universe. But he is also creative. With man, something new has appeared on earth and a new factor has been introduced into the evolutionary process. That process no longer goes along only according to its own inbuilt laws, for man begins to interfere with it and contributes to guiding it. Alongside biological evolution one has now to reckon with cultural evolution, which goes on at a progressively accelerating rate. Every theory of man has to take this novelty into account – the emergence of a *differentia* that separates him from the other creatures. We do not minimize the affinities between man and the animal creation, but we do not ignore the difference either. To quote J. Bronowski: 'The wonderful work on animal behaviour by Konrad Lorenz naturally makes us seek for likeness between the duck and the tiger and man; or B. F. Skinner's psychological work on pigeons and rats. They tell us something about man. But they cannot tell us everything. There must be something unique about man because otherwise, evidently, the ducks would be lecturing about Konrad Lorenz, and the rats would be writing papers about B. F. Skinner.'[22]

The Greeks found the distinctive characteristic of man in his reason. Reason is essentially the capacity for judgement. The bearer of reason can, as it were, step back from the immediate situation, even from himself, and make a reflective judgement. Traditional Christian theology has spoken usually of spirit. This is a word that has been used in many senses, but perhaps what is fundamental to it is that it indicates a capacity of the spiritual being to go out from himself, to 'proceed', to use theological language. This is a basic condition of creativity. The world of spirit is the world which man builds up through going out from himself and his immediate concerns. Modern existentialists have also seen the *differentia* of man in his 'existence', in the sense of 'going out', 'surging up' in the world (a favourite phrase of Sartre). Still another word that has become popular in modern theories of man and is now freely used among the more humanist Marxists is 'transcendence'. Man transcends the world in the sense that he makes it his object, but he also transcends himself in the sense that he is all the time passing over into new states and conditions of himself. As not merely creature but also creative, the creative creature or the created creator, man occupies a unique position. He continues to be subject to the laws of nature, yet he now increasingly imposes his own law on nature. For the first time a being has emerged whose future does not consist in adapting to natural conditions but in adapting natural conditions to himself.

As in the case of models of God and creation, attempts are often made to escape the tension of creatureliness and creativity by sacrificing one side to the other in the interests of a tidy theory. There are attempts (though possibly the twentieth century is showing itself less reductionist than the nineteenth) to bring man wholly within the realm of nature and to show that he is only a highly complex animal or mechanism of some kind, determined throughout his being by natural forces. Existentialism, which reacted against mechanistic and naturalistic views of man, has frequently fallen into the opposite error of so stressing the freedom, transcendence and autonomy of man that he is cut off from his roots in nature, and seems to be depicted in a vacuum rather than in a real world. Man is made the measure of all things. Sometimes, however, these opposing views tend to collapse into each other. The 'scientific' view of man as no more than part of the natural universe is often combined (whether consistently or not) with an optimistic humanism which urges man to constitute himself the arbiter of reality and value; while an atheistic existentialism, convinced of the futility of the human lot, may encourage a pessimistic resignation of freedom and a slipping back into the merely natural.

It would be a misunderstanding to suggest that the Christian doctrine of creation solves these dilemmas. In fact, Christian doctrine recognizes yet another complicating factor: sin. Ideally, man is the creature whom God has also made co-creator. Both man and nature are unfinished, and they move along now not simply under laws of nature, but toward goals which man has a share in setting. But because of sin, this is certainly no automatic progress. The sin may be the sin of pride. Just as God has been conceived on a monarchical model, so there is the monarchical understanding of man, a one-sided understanding of himself which accepts his freedom, autonomy and creativity, but neglects his limitations, dependence and createdness. The contrary sin is *accidie*, a combination of sloth and despair. This includes the desire to return to the womb (Freud), or to become mere flesh (Sartre). Man oscillates between them, and each in its own way poisons his relation to the world.

As for the biblical teaching that man was created in the image of God, we are aware that this image can be reversed so that man creates God in a human image, and we have in fact taken note that the monarchical model of God reflects to some extent the image of the earthly ruler. But if we are right in thinking that the Christian revelation of God as love requires qualification of the monarchical model, then when we think of man as made in the image of God, this qualification must be borne in mind. In much traditional theology, the image of God

in man was identified with man's 'dominion' over the earth
and the creatures in it: 'Then God said, ". . . let them have
dominion over the fish of the sea, and over the birds of the air,
and over the cattle, and over all the earth, and over every
creeping thing that creeps upon the earth" ' (Genesis 1:26).
The word 'dominion' essentially means 'lordship', and clearly
man does exercise lordship over the earth, and according to the
biblical teaching this is what God intended for him. But in
classical discussions of the meaning of 'dominion' (e.g. in John
Wycliffe) there was explicit criticism of the simple identification of dominion with mere sovereignty and the right to
dispose. True dominion, while it is a genuine power and lordship, is nevertheless, like the dominion of God himself, informed by love.[23] It is analogous to the ideal relationship of
the feudal lord to his vassals, in which he had responsibility for
their welfare as well as the right to their obedience; or, in
modern times, to that of an army officer to the man in his unit,
from whom he expects obedience to his orders and for whom
he is responsible. Thus if we speak of the dominion of man over
the world, this is not to be understood as ever having been a
charter for unrestricted exploitation. Man's dominion is given
to him by God and should be modelled on God's own dominion. If this is to be represented in monarchical terms, it is
the feudal ideal of responsible monarchy that is relevant, not
the conception of an arbitrary despot. Man should act responsibly towards nature, caring for the land (cf. Leviticus 25:1-5),
for domesticated animals (cf. Deuteronomy 25:4), and even for
wild life (cf. Deuteronomy 22:6).

Perhaps nowadays not 'dominion' but the term 'responsibility' is the one that is most adequate for referring to the
situation of man in the world and vis-à-vis the world. Responsibility can be assumed only by an adult. It applies to that con-

dition of man in which he has left behind not only the passive conformity to laws of nature such as is characteristic of the animal and material creation, but also that earlier period of human history when man was acutely aware of his absolute dependence and when his moral life was regulated by an externally given religious law. Yet responsibility does not mean complete autonomy, and certainly it does not mean the creation of values by man without regard to any objective structures of a moral natural law. Responsibility is an idea of almost inexhaustible depth, and leads into an ever-widening context. In the first instance, everyone is responsible to himself. This is part of the meaning of being a person, of being able to transcend oneself and project oneself, and, within limits, to choose what one shall become. But none of this takes place in isolation. I am responsible to society, for I cannot exist apart from it. I am engaged with others in co-operative work, in giving and receiving, and this also constitutes my transcendence of the immediate limits of my existence, making me part of a larger human entity. As we recognize very clearly today, this responsibility is not merely a horizontal one in the presently existing society, it is also a responsibility that extends through time: to the past, for I am responsible for the knowledge, techniques, wealth, cultural resources and all the rest that have been entrusted to this generation; and perhaps even more to the future, when we consider what kind of world we are going to leave for the generations to come. Furthermore, as space exploration goes on apace, it begins to be possible to speak of a cosmic responsibility. For example, has man an unlimited right to shoot his 'space probes' into the outer regions, without any clear knowledge of what the consequences might be?

If responsibility is an adult idea in the sense that it recognizes human freedom and the duty to make mature moral judgements, rather than merely follow laws authoritatively laid down, it must also be clear that responsibility is always responsibility to or before something. And if we ask, 'To what?' or 'Before what?' it soon becomes clear that one cannot circumscribe the area of responsibility. In the light of all we have said above about man's place as a creature in created nature, it follows that we must affirm that the responsibility must be understood and exercised as responsibility to God the Creator. This means joining with God as his co-workers. It implies both a respect for creation as a vast enterprise greater than man can understand and doubtless transcending human ends, and yet also the task of working on the creation to help bring forth its potentialities. A responsible attitude to the creation means that it is to be both appreciated and manipulated, and that each of these attitudes has to be balanced against the other. To take extreme examples, we are not *only* to gaze in aesthetic wonderment or *only* to exploit for economic advantage, but to learn the wisdom of rightly combining these attitudes.

Evil in Creation

In this chapter we have concentrated our attention on the doctrine of creation. But we have taken note that the creation, both of man and of nature, is an ongoing process, still unfinished, so that the good purposes of God in creation are still only on their way to realization. Furthermore, we have taken note of sin in human life, and, since man has a share in shaping creation, his sin is capable of perverting the enterprise from its goal, just as his responsible co-operation can help to realize its goal. We must now consider more carefully this negative and even distorting activity that is at work in creation. For man no longer encounters the creation as something given in a neutral way, still less as something unambiguously good. He finds himself already born into a society that has related in distorted ways to its environment, so that the environment itself has become distorted.

Confronted with the evils that appear in the environment itself, some Christian theologians have taught the doctrine of a cosmic fall. They have believed that not only has man fallen into sin, but that the entire cosmos is fallen. Calvin for instance wrote that the sin of Adam 'perverted the whole order of nature in heaven and earth'.[24] The more extreme forms of a doctrine of a cosmic fall, though they might claim some support from the Bible, are too speculative to command assent and involve ideas that are not readily harmonized with modern conceptions of the world. We mean doctrines which claimed that the world is subject to evil demonic powers. Historically, such beliefs have usually led into some form of Gnostic dualism. But, leaving aside the more extreme statements, we can acknowledge an important residual truth in the doctrine of a cosmic fall. There comes a point at which evils, which may have had their origin in the sinful will of man, become so entrenched in society and in the environment that they acquire a life and momentum of their own which may be called 'demonic'. There are superhuman dimensions of evil which neither individual men nor society as a whole seem able to control. Wars escalate beyond the intentions of the combatants, the arms race has got out of control, the less desirable aspects of technology proliferate in spite of us. These are only a few of the more obvious examples. Paul seemed to be aware of this problem when he pointed to the fact that man 'worshipped and served the creature rather than the Creator' (Romans 1:25), and as a result falls victim to powerful idols which take control of his life and pervert it. All these ideas get a new relevance today, when we have become aware that man can spread pollution through the environment – the air, the waters, the land and even outer space – and then finds that this pollution in turn threatens his own very existence. If man, as the creature who is also co-creator, is in constant interaction with his environment as a whole, if he is part of the intricately interconnected workings of the universe, then a disorder in man must produce some disorder in his environment. The theological theories of a cosmic fall hint at a kind of moral pollution. They suggest that man's sinful acts extend in their consequences far beyond what he normally supposes, and that they tend to frustrate and deflect the cosmos from whatever purposes of good God may have for it.

What has been said in the last paragraph is far from exhausting the problem of evil in the world. There are so-called 'natural evils' of suffering and waste that are not apparently attributable to man. It would be highly implausible to see, for instance, the habits of parasites and carnivores as results of man's sin, or all the sufferings that result from drought, plague, flood, earthquake, famine, etc. No doubt some of these matters belong to the unfinished state of creation and some to the conditions that necessarily belong to existence in an orderly physical universe, but there is a core which seems to place a question-mark against the doctrine of creation by a loving God.[25]

Because of the reality of sin and its consequences, together with those disturbing evils which seem to be of non-human origin, Christian theology does not teach simply a doctrine of creation, but links creation indissolubly to redemption and sanctification. Christianity is far from teaching any complacent easy-going doctrine that this is the best of all possible worlds. It teaches rather that God's potentially good creation needs to be redeemed and sanctified, and that these are costly processes. Creation, redemption and sanctification are not to be understood as successive activities on the part of God. Just as creation belongs not only to the beginning but is ongoing, so redemption is not only in the middle and sanctification not only at the end. Rather these are distinguishable aspects of God's unitary activity of creation-redemption-sanctification.

Christian responsibility for the creation before God might seem an impossibly demanding doctrine, were it not placed in this wider context of the doctrines of redemption and sanctification. These doctrines give man the assurance that, in spite of sin, absurdity and frustration will not have the last word. Man can take up his responsibility with hope, as co-worker with One who goes to the utmost lengths for the sake of his creation, and has power to open up new possibilities in every seeming dead-end.

3

THE SCOPE OF SALVATION

A Cosmic View of Salvation

We ended the last chapter by remarking that redemption takes place together with creation as God seeks to overcome every threat to his creation and to enhance the life of his creatures. It must be admitted however that, by contrast, the Christian view of salvation is usually regarded as basically moralistic and individualist. Jacob Needleman, in his interesting study, *The New Religions*,[1] suggests that it is precisely this lack of a cosmology which makes many of our contemporaries turn to such other religious traditions as Buddhism, Hinduism and Islam in order to find a way of life which offers a universal as well as a personal salvation. Catholicism and Protestantism alike, both in their popular teaching and in their pastoral practice, have concentrated on the salvation of individual souls. They have sometimes spoken of the salvation of society, but they have said little or nothing of man's place in nature. The efforts of some theologians such as Joseph Sittler[2] to assert a cosmic Christology have not so far resulted in any major change of attitude.

Western Christianity has often given a very negative impression of what is meant by salvation or redemption. Much has been said about sin, man's alienation from and his guilt before God. Little has been said about the action God takes to maintain his original purpose in the creation of the universe or about the final vision of transformation to which the process of redemption leads. It is as though the central element of a story has been isolated from its beginning and its end, and so has lost its essential meaning and interest.

Eastern Christian writers have seen the apparent narrowness of the Western view of salvation as one of the distinctive marks of the Western as opposed to the Eastern Christian tradition. Paul Verghese, for instance, in a recent book, *The Freedom of Man*,[3] traces back to St Augustine a number of features of the Western view of salvation which seem to him particularly unbalanced. He argues that Augustine's own character, and the historical circumstances in which he lived, led him to a dangerously unbalanced view of the sinfulness and hopelessness of man. From this there comes a failure to see what is implied in the idea of Incarnation for humanity and the material world. 'Regard the flesh, the body, matter as evil, or even inferior, and one has already begun the deviation from Christian faith.'[4] Another such element, mentioned in the previous chapter, is the view of man as 'abject dependant', according to which God can only be exalted at the expense of man. Yet another is the emphasis placed on the salvation of the individual, considered apart from his place in society and apart from human society's place within the whole created order. Linked with this again is too restricted a view of the nature of the sacraments. 'Without the recovery of a richer sacramental view, we cannot recover a theology which takes the incarnation seriously . . . Matter is the medium of the spirit. Indeed, matter is spiritual, so the Eastern fathers would argue. If theology is to do justice to technology and culture, a higher view of the sacraments is necessary.'[5] Undoubtedly these large assertions need further discussion and elucidation. It is evident that the thought of St Augustine himself is much wider and richer than these trends here outlined would suggest. But distinct traces of them can be found in his writings, and they certainly come to characterize much of Western Christianity.

The growing secularization of the world, and the rapid and increasing growth of scientific knowledge of the universe, have tended to increase this disjunction between the relation of man to God, on the one side, and his relation to the material world, on the other. It has not been and it is not now easy for the Christian tradition to adapt itself and grow so as to meet man's changing understanding of the world and of himself. The present moment nonetheless, though it offers a great challenge to the Christian tradition, also offers, as we shall suggest, unexpected possibilities of new understanding and openness between the scientific and religious areas of man's life. Furthermore, in our present human situation of approaching world crisis, past traditions of religious thought (both Christian and non-Christian) may have valuable insights for us. The fact that they are formulated in terms of world-views other than our own does not deprive them of their value. What seems to be becoming clearer is that for theology to accept its limitation to the realm of man's subjectivity is disastrously to narrow its scope. Either it must speak, however tentatively, about God the Creator, and all the things that he creates, or it can speak adequately about nothing, not even about man's subjectivity.

What would then be the characteristic of a cosmic view of salvation as seen within the Christian tradition, and how far would it be possible to restate it in terms which fit our own day? One answer to this would be to turn at once to the outstanding contemporary restatement in the work of Teilhard de Chardin. Whatever the limitations of his personal vision, the greatness of what he attempted must be acknowledged, and this is attested by the wide interest and influence that his writing has commanded. On the other hand his position has not escaped powerful criticism from a variety of viewpoints, both scientific and theological. Rather than concentrate our attention on a single author, it would perhaps be more helpful to sketch in some of the main outlines of that earlier Christian tradition which Teilhard re-expressed in sometimes idiosyncratic language. Taken in terms of Christian tradition as a whole, much of his thinking is far less isolated than is often supposed by critics who know only the theology of recent centuries.

A more positive view of salvation would rest upon a different view of God as Creator. It would begin with the faith that God created all things good, that he has made man in his own image and that, despite the reality of sin, the world and man essentially remain the good creation of God.[6] It would stress that, while the world is distinct from God and dependent upon him, it is not separated from him, nor he from it. It would maintain that God does not act arbitrarily. If he created of free choice and by deliberate decision, nonetheless he acts in accordance with his nature of love and for the increase of joy.

The Anglican theological tradition in these matters has its own distinctive character, which at least in some respects links it with the Eastern tradition.[7] For example, two typical and influential theologians of the nineteenth century, F. D. Maurice and B. F. Westcott, constantly affirmed that theology should not start from man's fall and his sinfulness, but from his creation in God's image and likeness. Richard Hooker, perhaps the greatest theological mind in post-Reformation Anglicanism, laid similar emphasis on the doctrine of creation. He insisted that God's decision to create is not arbitrary but in accord with the laws of his own being. 'They err therefore who think that of the will of God to do this or that there is no reason besides his will. Many times no reason known to us; but that there is no reason thereof I judge it most unreasonable to imagine . . .'[8] He taught that the world, although always distinct from God, participates in God and God in it, by its very being as his creation. Indeed, the ideas of participation and mutual indwelling in relation to God and the world, as well as to other matters, are key concepts in the whole of his system.

It has already been remarked that the emanationist model of creation, while it was rejected by the Church as heretical by itself, at the same time provides a useful corrective to the model of 'making' inasmuch as it suggests that there is a real sense in which God is in his creation. The fathers of the Church retained much that was positive in the emanationist view of things, particularly the sense of God's intimate involvement with the world at every level of its being. God is in all things by his creative power. All things are to be known and understood as 'words' of God, or as containing God's 'words', that is, his dynamic active intentions for men and for the whole of creation.

In such a universe, what Christian theology has called *the* Incarnation of the Word of God is not seen as an isolated wonder, but rather as the focus of a universal pattern of purposeful activity summed up and established at this point. 'The Word' of God, who is God, wills at all times and in all things to work the mystery of his incarnation', as Maximus the Confessor, one of the profoundest and most systematic of all the Byzantines, declared.

This view was, of course, worked out in terms of the worldview of classical Greece and Rome, a picture of the physical universe very different from our own. But it could perhaps be even better worked out in the context of our more historical and evolutionary view of the universe rather than in the more static world-picture of those days. To speak of things as being sacramental in such a view does not mean that they are a veil which hides the real world from us. It means that all things need to be seen in relation to one another, and that all things have inherent within them depths of meaning and possibility which are of indefinite extent. Such a way of looking at things is not in itself uncongenial to the contemporary scientific approach.[9]

If the Greek fathers held that it was essential to be able to distinguish things without necessarily separating them, and to unite them without necessarily confusing them, they did not do so merely from a desire for metaphysical subtlety, but because they believed that at the very heart of Christian experience man finds himself reconciled and united to God in a way which removes all barriers between him and his Creator but without annihilating him in the fire of the divine omnipotence. They wished to maintain, at one and the same time, what we understand today as the immanence and the transcendence of God; and to this end they developed a distinction, not altogether unlike that put forward by Whitehead and the process theologians, between God in himself and God in his energies. The world and man participate in the divine energies in which God comes out of himself in love for his creation; while God in himself remains always transcendent and unknown, beyond all participation.

This insistence on God's sovereignty has its basis in the Old Testament, and the strength of its affirmation in the fathers is a sign that patristic theology has strong biblical roots. But the stress on God's otherness does not imply that he is unconcerned for man and the world: quite the reverse. Because God is holy, man too is called to be holy and to embody this holiness not only in acts of worship in which he approaches God directly, but in all his daily life, in his relationships with other people, in the way he treats his animals, his tools and the earth. 'When you reap the harvest of your land, you shall not reap your field to its very border, neither shall you gather the gleanings after your harvest. And you shall not strip your vineyard bare, neither shall you gather the fallen grapes of your vineyard; you shall leave them for the poor and for the sojourner: I am the Lord your God . . . You shall not oppress your neighbour or rob him. The wages of a hired servant shall not remain with you all night until the morning. You shall not curse the deaf or put a stumbling block before the blind, but you shall fear your God: I am the Lord' (Leviticus 19:9-10, 13-14). God's concern and care spreads out into every detail of life, and all is seen in the light of his glory. The teaching of Jesus as depicted in the gospels in no way diminishes this sense that everything is in the hands of God, and the divine beauty is to be seen in the things that he has made. In fact any reflection on the language of the parables shows behind them a mind acutely aware of the value and meaning of everyday things.

On such a view of creation, although man is distinct from the rest of creation, he is by no means separated from it. All things, no less than man, have God as their Creator. The first of the covenants which God makes with man in the book of Genesis is that which follows on the Flood. It is made with all mankind and with all living creatures. 'While the earth remains, seedtime and harvest, cold and heat, summer and winter, day and night, shall not cease' (Genesis 8:22). Although in this covenant with Noah, the command to man to have dominion over the animal kingdom is repeated, it is clear that mankind is included with the whole living creation in a relationship of dependence upon God.

In the New Testament this conviction of man's solidarity

with creation is reasserted particularly by St Paul in his teaching that all things are summed up in Christ. This tradition continues on into the classical Christian formulas of worship. 'Earth and sky and sea and all things' are redeemed through the sacrifice of Christ. Many of the early eucharistic prayers contain lengthy thanksgivings for the whole material order, and for man's place within it. 'They confess in the face of paganism the world's original goodness, not as a theory of origins, but as . . . a programme and promise of action in obedience to God, who founded the world, the city and the Church, and gave man his vocation to turn the wilderness into a garden. They are not cosmogonies, but confessions of faith that Christ has conquered and that the world is good.'[10] It is true that man alone is made in God's image and likeness, and that he alone of all creation can make a free and conscious response to God's creative Word. But the special position which he holds, far from divorcing him from the world, gives him a special responsibility for it. If he is in some way the mediator between the world and God, he is able to be so because he is also in himself a microcosm, a little world, made up of elements of the material creation.[11]

The Desacralization of the World

It is clear that Western Christians during the last two centuries have not held this kind of view of God's creation and salvation. As our knowledge of the universe has grown beyond all comparison with the science of previous ages, so we have thought less and less of the physical world in terms of its relationship with God. The natural sciences became autonomous; the sphere of theology steadily contracted. For many people concepts such as 'mystery' and 'wonder' no longer seem appropriate in connection with the growth of scientific knowledge.

At the present time this development is being seriously questioned. From within the scientific enterprise itself there has come a new awareness of the mysteriousness, the unexpectedness of the universe. Harold K. Schilling, for instance, in his work, *The New Consciousness in Science and Religion*,[12] argues that there has been a radical change of attitude as between what he calls 'modern' and 'post-modern' science. 'According to the former view the world was closed, essentially completed and unchanging, basically substantive, simple and shallow, and fundamentally unmysterious – a rigidly programmed machine. The second regards it increasingly as unbounded, uncompleted and changing, still becoming, basically relational and complex, with great depth, unlimited qualitative variety, and truly mysterious . . .'[13] Indeed, one of the themes of Schilling's book is the reinstatement of the concept of 'mystery', which he analyses in depth, as of great value both in scientific and religious thinking. Such changes within the scientific enterprise in themselves do nothing to prove the validity of traditional religious viewpoints. They do however open up new possibilities of dialogue, and occasionally show remarkable examples of convergence between disciplines which have been long separated.

Meanwhile within the theological world the progressive desacralization of the world has come to be more deeply studied. The vast majority of theologians have come to welcome the fact that the sciences have developed in more and more complete independence of theology. There is no thought of trying to turn the clock back and reinstate the old ascendancy of theology. At the same time, within very recent years, something more of the ambiguities of the process of desacralization has begun to become evident. Men have begun to ask themselves seriously whether something important was not lost when the old sacral picture of the universe broke up. They have begun to ask themselves afresh whether this was an exclusively Western European phenomenon, and when it really began.

On these points there is an interesting convergence between theologians like Paul Verghese on the one side, and writers like Lynn White[14] on the other. The former is concerned from an Eastern Orthodox viewpoint to understand what is specific in the development of Western Christendom. The latter is in search of an answer to the question why the technological and scientific revolutions should have taken place in the West, and not in the Christian East. Both sides are inclined to feel that there are decisive differences between the two traditions in this area, and to put the moment of schism early rather than late. Verghese points to St Augustine. White speaks of the eighth or ninth century. Both suggest that by the high Middle Ages, the time of scholastic theology and the first developments of medieval science, the time also of the definitive split between the Eastern Church and Rome, the differences were already well established. The East was basically contemplative; the West became more and more activist. In the West, God is set over man, and man is set over the rest of creation as its active master and lord.

There is truth in this assertion, but it does not contain the whole truth. For the Western picture is less clear-cut. There are some signs that the old unitary view of creation and salvation maintained itself much later in the West. Renaissance and Counter-Reformation Catholicism contain splendid affirmations of the goodness of the material creation, and of its capacity for reflecting the divine glory. In England also, the view of a man as a microcosm and the vision of the whole world as potentially sacramental, full of God's presence, still survived. It received a striking statement in the preaching, poetry and theology of the writers of the first part of the seventeenth century. Only in the latter part of that century, under the impact of a new science and a new philosophy, did the old way of seeing the interrelationship of man's inner world with the world around him,[15] and of both with God, finally break down. Indeed, the English romantics, notably Coleridge and Wordsworth, made a remarkable if not wholly successful attempt to reaffirm it at the very time when, in the thought of Kant and Schleiermacher, religion was finally becoming restricted to man's subjectivity. From this has come a wealth of poetic writing which has helped greatly to maintain the vision of the world as potentially sacramental.

To return to the period before the Reformation and the Renaissance, it is clear that the old sacral view of the universe, although under pressure, was still powerfully present. Lynn White has asserted that the attitude towards creatures shown by St Francis was something altogether exceptional. Further reflection will hardly support this contention. Eloi Leclerc, for instance, in his remarkable analysis of 'The Canticle of the Creatures', has shown how much there is which is original in St Francis' presentation, and at the same time how much there is which is characteristic both of the Christian and of other religious traditions. 'By speaking of the subhuman realities of the world as our "brothers and sisters" we are at once introduced to a way of being present in the world wholly different from that which is marked by the will to dominate and possess things.'[16]

There is ample evidence to show that such an attitude towards nature, seeing it as something to respect and to cherish, as well as to employ, was still commonly found at this period.

An eloquent expression of it could be found for instance in the thirteenth-century Carmelite text called the *Ignea Sagitta*. 'All our sisters, the creatures, who in solitude charm our eyes or our ears, give us rest and comfort. In silence they give forth their beauty like a song, encouraging our soul to praise the wonderful Creator.'[17] It is a paradox which Leclerc considers at length in his study of St Francis' great song, that what begins with a movement towards God away from all the creatures continues with an affirmation of a passionate solidarity with all created things. St Francis was by no means the only saint renowned for his friendship with animals. Innumerable anecdotes, from all the periods of Christian sanctity, go to confirm the observation of our contemporaries, that people who are inwardly quiet, and without fear or aggression, can enter into remarkably intimate contact with the animal kingdom.

Certainly Christians, as Lynn White remarks, cut down many sacred groves. Like their Jewish and Moslem cousins they were resolutely opposed to anything which confuses the creation with the Creator, or simply identifies them both. But that is not to say, with Lynn White, that in the medieval West the universe had already been desacralized. There is continuity as well as discontinuity between pre-Christian cult and the Church's worship. The holy places of Christendom are frequently built upon the sites of earlier shrines; and many of the festivals take up pagan themes of the celebration of nature. Throughout the Middle Ages men thought of God as present in all his works, and believed that in their own activities they were co-operating with him. The churches which they built, the cities which grew up around them, the gardens which they planted, and the places where they chose to build their monasteries and shrines, all witness to this fact. Wherever such churches and such cities still exist, they act as a magnet to twentieth-century people,

who instinctively perceive in them the works of a society which
still saw a sacramental symbolism in man's co-operation with
God.[18]

Renunciation and Affirmation

It was in those ages that the monastic idea was widespread. This
idea took flesh in a way of life which expresses vividly something central in the whole Christian attitude to renunciation
and affirmation. At first sight it seems paradoxical to speak of
the monastic way in connection with affirming the goodness
of the world and of man's place in it. Monasticism, in popular
thought at least, involves flight from the world, the renunciation of possessions and of marriage, and of independent judgement and action. How can it be right to renounce what God
has made, and made very good? No less strange is the fact that
every Christian at the moment of his baptism has been called
upon to renounce the world, the flesh and the devil. This too
would seem a strange way of affirming that the world is inherently good.

The paradox of the renunciation of all things for God, and
the restoration of all things by God, is deeply rooted in the
Christian tradition. Man turns away from things to their
Creator, in order that from him he may receive them back,
restored, transformed. This is the movement of repentance
and conversion, the necessary preliminary to the life of faith.
We need to recognize, at the outset, that this can be a dangerous
paradox. The idea of renunciation can always be distorted in
the service of a tendency which sees the material world as
simply evil, to be rejected for its own sake. Though this view
has always been resisted in principle in the main line of Christian

tradition, it has, in practice, often been disastrously influential. On the other side we need to recognize that the paradox can also be life-giving. Throughout the history of Christianity, in different forms and in different situations, movements have arisen which involve a radical turning away from the world, and which yet give birth not only to deeds of compassion and love, but also to works of art and intellect of an outstanding quality. Only by losing his life can man save it. Only by rejecting the world can he truly find it.

What can these statements mean? Perhaps the example of the monastic renunciations, partly on account of their very unfamiliarity, can help us to see. At any rate we shall take them as an example, always remembering that they are only one way of working out a dialectic to which all Christians are, in one way or another, committed. If we can understand them aright they should throw light on the whole Christian situation, in the world and yet not of the world.

The renunciations of Christian monasticism have never been intended as ends in themselves. The vows of poverty, chastity and obedience are not to be made in an attitude of contempt or pure rejection. They are only the exterior of a positive movement towards God. As Kierkegaard saw, renunciation in this context does not imply a niggardliness on the part of God, as if he begrudges us the enjoyment of his creation. It signifies something much more liberating and mysterious, the possibility of entering into a direct relationship of love with God. This possibility is opened to us – as Kierkegaard remarked,[19] one could scarcely do it for oneself – to choose the Giver rather than his gifts. Having chosen him, and having been drawn into a relationship of faith and love with him alone, man finds that all the things that he had renounced are given back to him again, transformed because now they are seen and known precisely as God's gifts, words of God, full of his glory and his love. Men find themselves in a state best described as 'having nothing, and yet possessing everything' (2 Corinthians 6:10). The paradoxes of St Paul are reaffirmed throughout the Christian centuries, nowhere more powerfully than in the writings of St John of the Cross.[20] What has appeared as an affirmation of the worthlessness of the world becomes a supreme affirmation of its value and significance. The movement of withdrawal, of flight from the world, sometimes frightening in intensity, is crowned by a movement of return, whether in the case of Anthony in fourth-century Egypt, or of Seraphim of Sarov in nineteenth-century Russia.

In this way the monastic vows can assume a sudden and unexpected relevance not only to our twentieth-century fear that the world is without meaning or value, but also to the world's dawning crisis about the environment. This relevance has been perceived at least by some of the young, who have gone outside the conventional patterns of Western society and have attempted to re-invent the monastic life for themselves, often in one of its non-Christian forms. For the ecological problems of today stem from attitudes exactly the reverse of poverty, chastity and obedience. These contrary attitudes make men seize upon the world and destroy its worth in so doing. Possessiveness and grasping, exploitation and lack of respect, arrogant assertion of one's own immediate interests and advantage, characterize many of the features of contemporary society. These affect men's ways of dealing with things no less than men's ways of dealing with one another. Almost without thinking the language of rape and violation is used in speaking of man's misuse of the material world. The contemplative approach to things, which the other way of life promotes, requires a capacity to respect and to regard things in themselves: it demands a greater objectivity, and makes possible a different kind of enjoyment. /

/ The monastic vows, as we have already said, constitute only a particular way of living out the traditional vows of baptism, which all Christians have made, or have had made on their behalf, when first initiated into the way of salvation in Christ. For all Christians salvation is both from the world and for the world. It is salvation from the world as a self-enclosed system, which seems caught up in its own destruction. It is salvation for the world as a reality constantly open towards the light and energy of God, in which man is called actively to participate in the processes of creation. Evil, in Christian understanding, is profoundly ambiguous. On the one hand its seriousness and weight can never be denied: Jesus' death on the cross prevents that. On the other hand the power of evil can never be made equal to that of God. Faith in the Resurrection, no less than faith in God as Creator, always prevents that. Evil is seen in a great variety of ways, as a lack of completeness, as a distortion or disfigurement of something still good in itself, as an alienation or frustration of purposes which cannot find fulfilment, or as a state of separation in which men find themselves cut off from themselves and from one another, because they are cut off from the true source of their life in God. Evil is something out of which God can bring good; but it is never in itself purely and simply a step towards good. /

Often evil is seen in terms of possession, as if the world and men had fallen into the hands of some malevolent hostile power. This way of speaking is deeply rooted in the Christian tradition of prayer: 'Deliver us from evil'; 'Grant that we fall into no sin, neither run into any kind of danger.' It is a way of speaking curiously powerful in a time when many people feel themselves in the grip of forces over which they have little control. These ways of speaking may be useful and indeed necessary in helping us to understand the profoundly tragic situation in which man finds himself and the world in which he is placed. He is conscious on the one hand of the possibility of life and freedom, order and meaning; but he is also aware of the invading power of death and obsession, chaos and absurdity. There is something to be saved from, and something to be saved for; something to be renounced and something to be affirmed.

What is renounced is a turning in upon oneself and a turning in upon the world as something to be possessed and used in a self-regarding way. To renounce the world is to renounce the attitude of greed and grasping at things and people, which (as man experiences from childhood onwards) spoils his enjoyment and appreciation of things and people to be enjoyed. To renounce the flesh is to renounce the attitude which demands immediate returns in pleasure and prestige. Because it is basically self-centred, this attitude ignores the rights of others (both things and people) to their own existence. To renounce the devil is to renounce the power which inclines men to demand the immediate satisfaction of all their wishes, and which nourishes in them the illusion that they are the centre of the universe, and that all things are arranged around them and for them. Hidden behind these renunciations is the affirmation that all things exist in themselves as God's creatures, that man can contemplate and enjoy them, and that, in collaboration with the Creator, he can himself take part in their creation and transformation. Man finds his true liberty not in an attempt to assert his absolute independence of himself from God, from others and from things, but in the recognition of dependence 'upon God, upon everything else, and, indeed, upon everything that can be taken up out of the creative processes into the ultimate purposes of love. Dependence seems to be the one great hope of mankind, and to be the only promise which has any promise of real fulfilment.'[21]

Thus man is saved from the illusion of supposing that he himself, or the world in which he lives, is a self-enclosed, autonomous entity. Men are saved for life in a world in which they find themselves as children of the God who has called all things into being, fellow-workers with him in the trans-figuration of the universe. The life and teaching of Jesus, no less than his triumph over death, through death, reveal that God is at work in all things, healing and sanctifying, and that men can never act or understand aright until they learn to see them in this way. This means at once a recognition of man's limitations and finiteness, and of the limitations and finiteness of the world in which we are placed. When men have used up all the world's coal, then they have used up all the world's coal. When a species has been exterminated, then it has been ex-terminated. When a language has been allowed to die, it can still be studied from without, but it is no longer a living language. Judgement is at work in the affairs of men. At times the tragic and destructive powers in human life seem to reign supreme. Nature too has its dark and sinister aspects.[22] There is much that escapes all our attempts at explanation and justifi-cation. Faith in the One who underwent the experience of extreme dereliction on the cross will not allow us to under-estimate these things. But it will lead us to recognize that 'the grace of God, which always fills up that which is lacking and heals what is wounded',[23] is constantly at work in the world. Even in situations of utmost hopelessness, possibilities of re-demption and of new life open out in ways which we could never have foreseen. /

The Sanctification of Matter

The Christian tradition has always seen the activities of God as unfolding in ways which mysteriously correspond with the threefold character of God himself, Father, Son and Holy Spirit. Here again the models which have been used are many and diverse. In general the work of the Second Person has been seen as that of creating and restoring order (the Redeemer, the Word) and that of the Third Person as the principle of new life (the Life-giver, the Fulfiller). As we have already seen, in recent centuries this whole work of God has been less and less considered in relationship to the material creation. Indeed, throughout the tradition there has been a tendency to concentrate on man's final end in such a way as to disparage the importance of his present condition, and of the necessarily gradual stages by which he advances from it.

Moreover, the work of God as Creator has often been thought of in an unduly static way, as if God created once, long ago, making a universe fixed and unalterable. But there is no need to understand the tradition in this way. To affirm that there are principles of intelligibility and coherence in the very nature of being, that the universe is neither chaotic nor wholly without meaning, does not necessarily mean that these principles are fixed and unalterable. God's work of creating, no less than his work of redeeming and of sanctifying, is still going on, and man is called to participate freely in it. These lines of thought are being explored at present by the school of process theologians in the United States of America. But they are also characteristic of the work of, for example, Fr Dumitru Staniloae, one of the outstanding Orthodox theologians of our century. If, following ancient terminology, all things are thought of as 'words' of God, or as containing his 'words' or ideas, these words need not be conceived of as static or closed. They are words which evoke man's response, and which open up in the nature of things indefinite vistas of knowledge and understanding, and of transformation and fulfilment. Whatever line of research may be chosen, it always seems to lead further, and it is always revealing an indefinite number of links with other possible lines of research.

Here there is an interesting similarity between certain lines of theological reflection, and the actual experience of those conducting scientific research. Schilling makes the point vividly by asserting that the more we know, the more we find that we do not know. 'In the history of scientific discovery every answer to a question about nature gives rise to more questions, and the answer to each of these to still others, and so on in a diverging series of more and more questions. If the world were a closed finite system, one would expect convergence in the long run, and science would eventually run out of anything to ask. But nothing whatever in the experience of science indicates that there is such convergence.'[24] To assert that the world is the creation of an infinite God who is constantly at work in it is precisely to assert that the world is open-ended. It is not finally closed in upon itself, but full of indefinitely numerous possibilities of growth, possibilities of new co-operation by man with God.

The affirmation that man is called to work together with God is particularly important at a time when men are more and more conscious of their capacity to change things, whether for good or for ill. This capacity, in theological terms, should be seen as a call to man to be co-creator with the Creator and to work out his own salvation in partnership with the Redeemer.

Christian faith does not imply that man's role in the world is passive. But no more does it imply that he is sole master of a world from which God, if there is a God, has absented himself.

The affirmation that God is at work in the world is involved in a faith in Christ as Redeemer. It is still more strongly implied in the faith that God the Holy Spirit is the giver of life. The earlier Christian writers who reflected on this subject often interpreted the Holy Spirit in terms of the multiplicity, variety and richness of creation, and as indicating the supreme freedom of God, who transcends any ideas or models which men may make of him. More recent Orthodox theologians develop this theme further.[25] The Holy Spirit is seen in relation to all expressions of human creativity and freedom and to all that is spontaneous and inexplicable; for example, to the products of artistic genius, and to man's capacity to transcend situations of great suffering. This must be further extended to the products of technological genius. Where the Holy Spirit is most active, there man is most free and most himself. Here too there is a play of an indefinite number of possibilities, an affirmation that the nature of the world is anything but fixed and closed. Growth and life, no less than consistency and order, are signs of the activity of God. Growth in personal life is unpredictable because it is a continual self-transcendence in freedom.

In thinking thus of the Holy Spirit a distinction must be made between a theory such as vitalism, and belief in the immanence of God. The former explains the development of one organism into another by the postulation of an added factor: a life-force or *élan vital*. But most biologists see no need for any such extra factor to explain the phenomena of life. Vitalism as a theory has been superseded by advances in physical, chemical and biological explanation. Again, if we speak of the world as full of the energies or activities of God, it is clear that we are using the word energy in a different sense from that in the statement 'Matter is a form of energy.' To speak in terms of the creative activity of God is to offer an interpretation of the world from the vantage-point of faith; to offer a unifying vision of reality, in which the power of God who brings it into being is seen as dynamically present within it.

The Holy Spirit is to be understood above all as God in his world leading men forward towards a fulfilment which as yet they can neither understand nor grasp. In the passage of the Epistle to the Romans where St Paul wrote of the world as in the pangs of new birth (Romans 8:22), he wrote also of the Holy Spirit as the one who gives a foretaste of the things to come (cf. Ephesians 1:14). At the heart of Christian worship men not only look back with thanksgiving to what God has done in the past, but they also look forward in the power of the Spirit to the Kingdom which is yet to come. 'Earthly bread and wine become the heavenly manna and the new wine . . . elements of the first creation become pledges and first fruits of the new heaven and the new earth.'[26]

The last quotation serves to remind us again that a 'richer sacramental view'[27] might also serve as a framework for our thinking about the relation of God-created man to God-created matter. In the traditional Christian understanding, the world of matter has the symbolic function of expressing God's mind and the instrumental function of being the means whereby he effects his purposes; and these functions also constitute the special character of the use of matter in particular Christian sacraments. In these sacraments there is a universal reference to this double character of created physical reality, and so meaning can be attached to speaking of the created world as sacramental, although this character is implicit, obscure and partial, rather than explicit and open, because of man's incomplete vision and because of evil. The sacramental character of the created order only becomes fully explicit in the life, death and resurrection of the God-incarnate human person of Jesus and in the new understanding and valuation of the very stuff of the world which is entailed in the eucharistic tradition of his commands at the Last Supper. This eucharistic tradition from the earliest times involved both a thanksgiving for creation and an offering (oblation) of creation by man back to God in the form of bread and wine which, significantly in the present context, are the product of man's work acting upon a familiar part of the natural world, corn and grapes. /

The Christian sacramental understanding of the material universe is congruent with the contemporary scientific perspective on the evolution of the cosmos from inorganic matter, through living organisms, to man. For each successive aggregation and coalescence of matter, as the cosmic development has proceeded, has clearly led to more complex forms assembled from simpler units, in accordance with the regular processes of natural laws. Yet with each complex form of matter, new qualities emerge in this sequence, including the behaviour and activity of living organisms in general, and, in particular and most notably, the conscious and self-conscious activities of human persons in all their baffling variety and self-creativity. In man, matter has become aware of itself and of its past, and has now become the controller and arbiter of the destiny of other forms of terrestrial matter – and, more tragically, has become aware of the paradox of its unfulfilled potentialities. But the Christian gospel is that man's potentialities *are* capable of fulfilment 'in Christ'. In the eucharist man offers himself to God, in unity with Christ's own self-offering, to co-operate in God's own creative work in the actual physical world. The consecration of the eucharistic elements is matched by and interwoven with the consecration of the participants so that they too become through the sacrament the means whereby they fulfil God's purposes for his world.[28]

The Last Things

As with Christian beliefs about salvation, so with Christian beliefs about the end of all things it must be admitted that much recent teaching has been individualist and moralistic. An inflexible doctrine of rewards and punishments after death was one of the foundation-stones of popular religion in early nineteenth-century England, and one of the principal causes of the moral revulsion from the Christian tradition which drove many people into agnosticism. To an unacceptable notion of an act of creation having taken place just over six thousand years ago there corresponded an equally unacceptable notion of a day of judgement, in which the greater part of mankind would be consigned to eternal torments. The doctrine of the end of all things, no less than the doctrine of their origin, had become disastrously narrowed and reduced. In eschatology as much as in creation we need a variety of images or models to speak of a reality which transcends any one way of conceptualizing or imagining it.

The New Testament and the Christian tradition have two principal and strongly contrasted ways of speaking about the end. On the one side there is the picture of judgement, a final separation of good from evil, the deliverance of all that is against the will of God to the fire. This strand of judgement is powerfully present in the New Testament writings, and it is one of the sources of the stress upon decision in the Christian understanding of human life. But on the other side there is also a hint, and at times more than a hint, of the restoration of all things, a promise of universal salvation, when God shall be all and in all and when not only mankind but all creation will be caught up into a new heaven and a new earth. The gospels, which speak so clearly of judgement, also assert that 'even the hairs of your head are all numbered', that 'not the least lash' (Gerard Manley Hopkins) will be lost, but that all will be found again in God's kingdom. The key category in the synoptic gospels is the Kingdom of God, when God's will shall be done on earth as in heaven, and all creation respond to his sovereignty and will.

In its developed form the doctrine of the restoration of all things corresponds to a doctrine of creation of the emanationist type. All things come forth from God; all things in the end return to him. It was Origen who seems to have been greatly attracted by such a view; and again the mind of the Church rejected it. For, taken in a literal and mechanical form, such a doctrine takes away the necessity of choice from human life, makes no allowance for the tragic element in experience, and ignores the whole of traditional language about judgement. But just as a rejection of an emanationist view of creation did not involve the loss of all the elements of truth contained in it, so, at least in some strands of Christian tradition, the model of final judgement has always been qualified by a model of a final restoration. Indeed, to speak only in terms of judgement is in the end as unbalanced as to speak only in terms of universal salvation. To build the frustration of God's loving purposes into the nature of things is to destroy the very hope that God will be all in all. So the Eastern Church has not ceased to teach that men may pray that all will be saved and that the whole created order will be transfigured by God's glory. These two pictures must be held together, for man is unable to resolve this antinomy whose solution lies beyond space and time. The possibility of maintaining such a tension is not only found in the Christian East. It is a remarkable characteristic of the teaching of Julian of Norwich in fourteenth-century England. (The words 'All shall be well' recur frequently in her book, *The Revelations of Divine Love*.)

To speak thus of the restoration of all things involves the whole creation and not mankind alone. On any interpretation of the classical Christian teaching about the resurrection of the body, it is difficult to see how man's bodily life can enter into eternity (and man's life is an aspect of his body, not an 'additional factor' added to it) without in some sense involving that world in which we have rejoiced and of which the human body is a part. Nothing which God has made will ultimately be lost. All the splendour of the natural world and the creative achievements of man, however transitory and easily destructible they may appear, have eternal significance.

Such language is clearly imaginative, containing a richness of meaning which cannot easily be analysed in prose. In speaking of the end of all things, as when we speak of their first beginning, we are brought to 'the edges of language'. We have to use stories, images, truth-telling myths. The last book of the Bible speaks in such ways of the lake of fire and the abyss, of the heavenly city which comes down from God, and of the river and the tree of life, whose leaves are for the healing of the nations. There are many unanswered and apparently unanswerable questions. What of all the suffering, misery and waste of human experience? What of the vast expanses of the physical universe and the apparently random prodigality of the evolutionary process? Does this vision include *all* the dinosaurs and *all* the mackerel that have ever been? The very asking of the question sugegsts limitations of language which must be observed in speaking of the Last Things. The image of the restoration of all things cannot be pushed to its literal conclusions. But then no more can the image of the Last Judgement, with its suggestion of discrimination between what is lasting and what is ephemeral, and its implication of a destruction of what is of no value. Both models are necessary and each complements the other. Both become ultimately more illuminating and acceptable when they are seen in conjunction with each other and when they are seen to apply not merely to man but also to the whole universe of which man is a small but important part.

4
FROM THEOLOGY TO ETHICS

Theological Insights

In the earlier chapters an attempt has been made to present the outlines of a Christian perspective within which today's world situation can be properly viewed. Obviously in the brief compass of these chapters only an outline could be presented, but we have tried to show, for the purpose of this report, the most important and relevant features of the Christian doctrines of creation, salvation and sanctification. People commonly think of these religious doctrines as applying primarily to the inner life of the individual. This is true up to a point. Each individual human being is a unique creation deriving his being from God; each, we believe, is of concern to God and to each is offered salvation, as deliverance from alienation through the restoration of a right relationship to God; and each has an ultimate destiny. But it is a mistake to understand Christianity in exclusively individualist terms. Christian doctrine has implications for the broad social and ethical problems that are raised by the environmental crisis. Loss of belief about the nature and destiny of the world and the substitution for it of interiorized and subjective forms of religion have gravely weakened the Christian Church, and have helped to make its teachings seem irrelevant to the problems of contemporary society. What we must attempt in this present chapter therefore is to draw out some of the implications of Christian

65

doctrine for responsible behaviour toward nature and the environment generally. We recognize too that individual efforts, valuable though they are, must be somewhat ineffective in the face of such gigantic problems, so that public opinion has to be mobilized and there must be pressure for such legislative and other controls as are needed.

This report is, of course, concerned with nature as it is known on this planet and with life as it has emerged in this terrestrial environment. It is thought not improbable by many nowadays that elsewhere in the universe other forms of life have emerged or will emerge. Since there are as yet no means of knowing anything directly about such other forms of life, we cannot say anything about them. Nevertheless, it is important to bear the possibility of such forms of life in mind, for it will save us from taking too narrowly anthropocentric a view of the material universe. It is certainly Christian belief that man has an important place in the purpose of God, but this is not to say that the universe has no other purpose than to be the setting for man's life or that it exists solely for man's benefit. It could well be that man is part of some much vaster enterprise in space and time than he yet understands, and this possibility carries obvious practical consequences for human attitudes to the universe.

Creation, salvation and sanctification are interrelated activities of the one God who is at work concurrently in all three modes. He is at work both in nature and in man. What is the relation between them? Although the Bible has no word for nature nor any concept that could be considered as closely comparable to the modern concept of nature, it does presuppose a fairly clear idea of non-human created reality. This is contrasted not only with man, who has dominion over it, but with God, and in this respect Hebrew religion was in sharp contrast to most of the so-called nature religions of the ancient world. In these nature religions, mountains, streams, the heavenly bodies and so on were divinized. But in Hebrew religion, they were deprived of any divine status, for they were the works of the one creator God. Over against God, man and nature were both seen as creatures. But man held a privileged position in the creation, for he was made in the image of God and to him God had committed control over nature. However, the arbitrary and reckless misuse of power by man proceeds not from the divine purpose but from human sin. God's purpose was that man should live in harmony with nature as well as with his fellow-men. The Old Testament envisaged an end-time when man would live in perfect harmony with the other creatures, and this may have been conceived as the restoration of a 'golden age' at the beginning of time, before man's fall into sin. For everything that God had made he judged to be good. Although it cannot be denied that man is very much at the centre of biblical teaching on creation, this teaching does not hold that nature has been created simply for man's sake. It exists for God's glory, that is to say, it has a meaning and worth beyond its meaning and worth as seen from the point of view of human utility. It is in this sense that we can say that it has an intrinsic value. To imagine that God has created the whole universe solely for man's use and pleasure is a mark of folly. The wise man will be able to read lessons for human behaviour from his observation of nature. Although in the New Testament there enters a note of apocalyptic pessimism, it remains true that the world as God's creation is in essence good. This natural world is not corrupt in itself (as Gnostics and some others held) but is in bondage to the powers of darkness, from whose grasp it can be delivered. God has a redeeming purpose for the whole creation, for nature as well as man. This, we would claim, is the teaching of the main-stream of biblical thought.

This mention of the 'mainstream' of biblical thought makes clear (as is done elsewhere in the report[1]) that there is no closely reasoned systematic theology of nature to be found in the Bible. It is possible to discover in its pages more than one theological viewpoint on these matters. In any case, it would be naïve to imagine that a blueprint for modern living could be read out of a few biblical texts coming from a very different cultural milieu. We live in an age far removed from biblical times. A return to pre-industrial society is not desirable, even if it were possible. Man has advanced very greatly in his under-standing of nature and in his power to control it. This new knowledge and power constitute the progressive realization of man's dominion. But clearly the new knowledge and power confront him with very difficult choices and decisions. The power and the knowledge are in themselves good. What must be questioned are the uses to which man has put them. No general statement can be made from the Bible about technological issues of great complexity, but this much can be affirmed on the basis of the biblical testimony. The theological affirmation that God is the giver of all wealth leads to warnings about human greed and about the need to care for the weaker members of a society; and in the same way the parallel affir-mation that God is the creator of all things leads to similar warnings that unless man respects the animal creation and the land from which he gets his food, his own future will be in jeopardy.

Insights from Non-Christian Sources

As Christians, we are of course concerned with the specifically Christian attitude towards man in relation to his environment. But we wish to be open to any insights that may come from other religions. No one has yet undertaken the vast work of a systematic study of attitudes to nature in the great religions of the world. But a few comments may be made here on the information available.[2] It is often claimed that Eastern religions have preserved a healthier attitude to nature than has Christianity, at least in its Western forms. If this is true, then Christians must welcome the fact, and have no need to be defensive about it. They must rejoice to find truth wherever it may be had, and it is a perversion of Christian faith to claim that truth is confined exclusively to the Christian dispensation. At the same time, the claim about the superiority of Eastern attitudes to nature is one that has to be subjected to careful scrutiny. The relation of religion to culture is always complex. Eastern religions reflect a pre-industrial outlook on life, and it may be a kind of nostalgia that makes some modern Western men turn to them in the hope of escape from the complexities of technological society. Some Eastern religions are fundamentally pessimistic in outlook, so that it is hard to assert that their concepts of the world are *better*. They often reflect a view of time that is cyclical rather than linear, thus denying an ultimate goal to the world-process. Even the concept of *ahimsa* (non-violence) has its roots as much in a doctrine of reincarnation as in any inherent benevolence. In some faiths animals are not merely reverenced but worshipped as divine beings. In such religions there may be a blurring of the distinctions between God, man and the world. In practical terms, it may well be true that adherents of Eastern religions have enjoyed a better working relationship with the natural world than some adherents of Western Christianity. In some ways, that has not been difficult, when one considers the enormous preoccupation of the West with industry and the corresponding absence (until very recently) of the temptation toward excessive industrial exploitation in the East. This implies in turn that these better practical attitudes in the East may have very little to do with inherently better beliefs about nature. Yet when all this has been said, it remains probable that the Eastern religions (and Eastern Christianity as well) have maintained a more contemplative attitude toward the natural world than has Western Christendom. It is not easy to determine, however, how far this contemplative attitude has theological roots in a particular religious faith, and how far it is typical of any pre-industrial society.

As well as inquiring about the attitudes to nature in non-Christian religions, it is worthwhile to ask about attitudes in professedly atheistic cultures. It is claimed, for instance, that the Chinese People's Republic has had success in coping with ecological problems. We are told that intermediate technology has been encouraged, recycling of resources introduced, measures taken to preserve the fertility of the soil, the rate of population increase curbed, and the dignity of manual labour upheld, even to the extent of requiring administrators and professors to work with their hands for a period each year. Many reasons can be given for this state of affairs. To some extent, it may be the result of lessons learned through the problems that have befallen other societies. To some extent, also, it is due to the fact that China is still only on the way toward industrialization, so that the full effects (and full temptations) of the industrial society have yet to be experienced. The measures introduced are made possible partly because the decrees of a severely authoritarian government can override the freedoms and idiosyncrasies of individuals in a highly collectivized totalitarian state, and in the democracies of the West it would go against the grain to give the state such powers. On the other hand there has also been at work among some of the Chinese the enthusiasm engendered by a common faith in what Marxism-Leninism can do for China. This point is important in showing the role which can be played by the visions arising from both theology and secular ideologies in inculcating good attitudes. The key Marxist doctrines of man, work and society, in so far as they are relevant to the environmental question, are examined elsewhere in this book.[3] It is also important to note that the claim is made that, under the influence of a common vision, Chinese citizens are able to forgo individual satisfactions for the sake of the common good. It is claimed, whether truly or not, that they have in the pursuit of corporate goals been able to renounce personal greed.

To the extent that Marxism is seeking the betterment of human society, it must also be concerned with that natural environment on which society depends for its very life. In the same way, scientific humanism, in attempting to promote human values, cannot fail to lay stress on the natural environment, for it is from this that men derive much happiness and satisfaction. But neither system proposes a view of nature as having any value and significance in itself which is not connected with utility. Traditional Marxism and much humanism are essentially anthropocentric. It is worth noting, however, that there are many types of humanism. Roger Shinn makes a useful distinction between the 'closed' humanism for which man is the measure of all things and an 'open' humanism which is much less dogmatic in character and acknowledges elements of mystery in the universe.[4] It remains to be seen whether new forms of Marxism and humanism will develop, stressing not only the duty of beneficence towards one's neighbour but also encouraging respect for the non-human created world, and doing so without acceptance of belief in a Creator and the duty to love him. It is at this point that we see a major difference between Christianity and the Marxist and humanist points of view. Christian faith views the non-human universe as the work of a loving personal Creator. It can be argued that some such belief is required if we are to have a right attitude toward that non-human reality, and if the evil exploitative tendencies in man are to be overcome. It is a matter of getting our priorities straight; that is, seeing the world as God's before we see it as given by him to us.

Contemporary Frustrations

But committed Christians now form a minority, and Western society has scarcely any common belief remaining about the origin, nature and destiny of man. There remain only the splintered relics of that unifying vision which belonged to our Christian inheritance. 'Where there is no vision, the people perish.' It is commonly said that man cannot control the industrial juggernaut that he has created, and we have daily evidences of how powerful forces that were once under human control seem now to have acquired a momentum of their own and to be dragging us along whether we like it or not. How could it be otherwise, if man no longer has any clear belief about who he is or any vision of the direction in which he wants society to develop? Unfortunately man will use his powerful new weapons in industry and agriculture to do violence to the world of nature, if he does not know what his relation to that natural world should be. Western man needs a belief-system, a system of myths and symbols, to interpret to himself his place in the world, his relationship to nature, his aims, his hopes, his foes and his friends. His new-found knowledge and powers make such a comprehensive world-picture more than ever necessary. But he has lost it.

In place of a unifying vision, we find ourselves nowadays confronted by what may be called a new secular moralism. The ethical demands of environmentalists fall constantly on the ears of the contemporary person, but he is very confused about them. To some extent he is sympathetic, to some extent negative. There is a part of him which joins in raising these questions, and there is a part of him which dismisses them.

'The population of the world is exploding, and even with bare replacement rates of reproduction, numbers will continue to increase because of the age structure of the existing population. Should we not be doing something about this?' But why worry? If there is disaster, it will strike the next generation and not ours. We really cannot control people's fertility. Why should they not be free to raise as many children as they may?

'We are using up non-renewable resources to the detriment of posterity. Should we not be doing something about this?' But previous generations never worried about us. Science will find a way out of the difficulties, as it always has done in the past. It would be wrong to stop the onward march of technological progress because of fears about what may happen in the future.

'We are perpetrating monstrosities of scale in agriculture, transport, housing, commerce and industry. Ought we not to stop such monstrosities?' But how else is it possible to feed the hungry, house the homeless, and provide the benefits of affluence that economies of scale can confer? The economic needs of man must take precedence over the aesthetic satisfactions of beauty and proportion.

'We are doing violence to nature by imposing our will upon it instead of using its natural restraints to promote human welfare. Ought we not to change course?' But human beings have always imposed their will on nature ever since they learned the use of fire, and now we have knowledge and techniques to enable us to master nature in far more efficient ways.

'We are exterminating species of living creatures by the selfish and unthinking slaughter of animals for our own use and pleasure, and for the indulgence of luxurious habits of eating and dress. Surely this ought to be stopped?' But in the process of evolution it has always been the case that some species of animals are passing out of existence and joining the vast number that have become extinct. We are only hastening a natural process.

'We are endangering the future by a perilous and imprudent expansion of the production of energy from nuclear fission. Ought we not to abandon this?' But man has always taken risks, regardless of the future. We must have energy, or modern culture will collapse, and at the moment nuclear fission looks like the best bet.

'We are overburdening our minds and bodies by the increasing stress and tempo of life, with attendant stress illnesses. Ought we not to change our life-style?' Yet statistically we are healthier than our forefathers. Diseases common in their day are now rare, and expectancy of life has greatly increased. These are the best criteria.

'We are dehumanizing life by the impersonal structures of

modern society, by our addiction to socially destructive tools, by an obsession for consumer goods, many of them useless, unnecessary and even unwanted. Ought we not to be putting the needs of people and the cultivation of personal and communal relations before our insatiable desire for things?' But mass-production methods are essential if goods are to be produced for all, and why should goods be produced unless the masses want them? If this is what people want, then this is what they should have.

But is this what people really want? Many people are confused about the way they live, as we have tried to show in the previous paragraphs. On the one hand, they rebel against what is happening. On the other, they persuade themselves that it is all inevitable. There is a good deal of fatalism at present. Droughts, famines, floods and epidemics still move people to respond to appeals from charities for help; but many are beginning to realize that, however efficiently modern technology can be used to alleviate suffering, such aid only palliates the symptoms of deeper ills. These ills inevitably result from the increasing application of present Western industrial and agricultural technology and from present Western styles of life which are spreading over the globe. People feel that there is something deeply wrong about them. They are ill at ease; and for all the conveniences of twentieth-century living, they know how hard it is to live a satisfying human life. Many of those who accept the list of answers outlined above hardly know why they do so. In any case they have little freedom of choice. They must either attempt to drop out of society (which is impossible) or conform. We have already noticed that individualist efforts can be of little avail. We have to go on living much as we do, unless and until society as a whole adopts a very different way of life. In traditional language, we are undergoing judgement, and experiencing the call to repentance, to a turning around of our values and policies.

Thus today's secular moralism is frustrating and in the end unacceptable. Our attitudes are moulded by what we believe, and the ethical demands of our age can be met only if there take place radical reappraisals of the nature, significance and destiny of man's life in the world, and these reappraisals must take place in society as a whole. This is not to say that there is no place for individual action. Groups of Christians and others, living in community and 'renouncing the world, the flesh and the devil', constitute both a sign of the future and a witness to it. Perhaps in our time there can be a new relevance for the religious life, which, in one of its aspects, can be seen as a 'sign of contradiction' in face of the affluent society of maximum production and consumption. However, it may be a symptom of the ascendancy of the consumer mentality not only in society at large but even in the churches that the membership of most religious orders has so sharply declined in recent years. But while individuals and groups, through their witness and example, can do something to help, they do not provide a final solution to the problems of the developed world, with all its vast complexity and interrelatedness. Thus we say that there must be a change of outlook in society as a whole. In the past society has been able to escape the necessity for such a radical change by finding fresh technological solutions for its problems. But it would seem that there are limits to the possibility of such solutions, because there are limits to growth itself. Now man is coming within sight of the ultimate limits of the planet in terms of population, resources and pollution; or, rather, he is approaching the points where decisions will be made which may lead to severe ecological crises. Man's alienation from his true nature and the dehumanizing effects of his present life-style are beginning to show themselves in alarming ways, and, as they do so, they are throwing into clearer relief the choices confronting him.

Hope for the Future

Already some shifts in public attitudes are becoming apparent. Education has to play its part in accustoming people to the changes that are becoming necessary. Perhaps it has first to wean people away from those rising expectations of increased consumption and comfort that have been so assiduously encouraged over the past decades. But re-education is not enough. Society as a whole will only adopt a different style of living if it has come under the impulse of a popular and imaginative way of seeing things in their wholeness. Such a vision needs more than a secular ideology. We believe that it can come about only through the agency of a theology, that is to say, through man's understanding of himself as a creature who finds his true being in a relationship of love with God and in co-operation with God in his purposes for the world. Such a self-understanding encourages in turn its own realization in act. Men are led to see themselves and then to act as God's stewards or trustees in the created order, so far as we know it.

To accept God as the Creator of all things implies that man's own creative activity should be in co-operation with the purposes of the Creator who has made all things good. To accept man's sinfulness is to recognize the limitation of human goals and the uncertainty of human achievement. To accept God as Saviour is to work out our own salvation in union with him, and so to do our part in restoring and recreating what by our folly and frailty we have defaced or destroyed, and in helping to come to birth those good possibilities of the creation that have not yet been realized. To 'renounce the world, the flesh and the devil' is to turn from grasping and greed and to enjoy people and things for their own sake and not because we possess them. To accept the Christian doctrine of the Resurrection is to persevere in spite of setback and disaster, to resist the temptation to slip into a mood of fatalistic resignation, to believe that success can be attained through failures and so to live in hope. To accept God as the Sanctifier of all things implies a respect for all existence, which is upheld by his Spirit and instinct with his energy. To accept our nature as created in God's image and likeness and as destined to grow toward him involves responsible use of those godlike powers over the natural environment which God has put into our hands. To hold that God has created the world for a purpose gives man a worthy goal in life, and a hope to lift up his heart and to strengthen his efforts. To believe that man's true citizenship is in heaven and that his true destiny lies beyond space and time enables him both to be involved in this world and yet to have a measure of detachment from it that permits radical changes such as would scarcely be possible if all his hopes were centred on this world. To believe that all things will be restored and nothing wasted gives added meaning to all man's efforts and strivings. Only by the inspiration of such a vision is society likely to be able to re-order this world and to find the symbols to interpret man's place within it.

We believe that such affirmations as these are necessary if there is to come about the radical shift of attitudes (*metanoia*, change of mind and heart, repentance) which society must achieve if our present ecological problems are to be solved instead of getting worse. Such a reorientation could eventually bring to an end the promotion of collective envy, greed and covetousness which influence all sections of a modern consumer society. In their place we would cultivate the less spectacular but essential virtues of equity and temperance, thrift and generosity. Instead of using human knowledge to do violence to nature, we would develop rather an attitude of respect toward nature, in which our knowledge is used to co-operate with natural restraints in order to achieve our desired results. Of course, these 'desired results' themselves would be transformed in the changing of attitudes throughout society.

In the past, such changes of attitude might have been thought desirable, but it is now becoming apparent that they are essential if man is to live at peace not only with his fellow human beings but also with the natural environment on which he depends for his life. Religious perspectives, far from becoming an optional extra in a secular society, are likely to be the vital means of society's salvation. For these changes in attitudes, values and policies will not come about otherwise than through the deep pervasive influence of a world-view which ties together men and nature in a unity, and which we believe will also lead society as well as individuals to acknowledge their accountability before God for their stewardship and trusteeship of the world. Here we again stress the importance of deep commonly held convictions as the precondition for imaginative and effective policies.

We are well aware of the interaction between man's attitudes toward his fellow-men and his attitudes toward nature. In Western society (and, for better or worse, its attitudes are gradually spreading over much of the globe) man not only finds himself out of harmony with the natural environment, but often finds himself in a wrong and frustrating relationship to his fellow-men, and also to his work, his tools and his artefacts. All these matters are interconnected. The relation between greed and aggression is too obvious to require comment, but probably all forms of alienation are subtly connected and each aggravates the other.[5] It is our conviction that these problems can be overcome only through the influence of a unifying vision of God's purposes for his world. Man can be brought into a proper relationship with all the entities with which he has to do when he sees himself not only as a member of the human family, nor just a part of the natural order, but also as a child of God.

We are aware too that in modern societies economic, social, environmental and political factors are all intricately inter-related, and that national decisions and events acquire inter-national importance. We therefore acknowledge that much expert knowledge (which we do not possess) is necessary before any significant new technological, political or economic de-cisions can be taken. The full significance of the present report could be made visible only by going on to relate it to some of the central problems of the environmental crisis, such as the problems of energy, food production and population. (At least some of our members believe that the population problem is the most fundamental and the one most bristling with diffi-culties of all kinds.) We believe that by relating these practical problems to the theological issues discussed in this report, it would become very clear how theological convictions can change attitudes and eventually affect policies.

It is sometimes suggested that, while not claiming to work out detailed solutions of practical problems, the Christian Churches ought to be in a position to lay down general prin-ciples derived from theological insights, so that these could be applied by experts to particular cases. Examples of such prin-ciples might be the value put upon each individual human life, which might be applied to forbid abortion, or capital punishment, or euthanasia; or the value put upon some higher animals, which might be applied to forbid hunting, or rearing battery chickens, or to encourage vegetarianism; or the Genesis injunction to multiply upon the earth and subdue it, which has been held to be an encouragement to unbridled exploitation of nature. But we have not thought it right to try to derive any such general principles from the theological insights we have discussed. As these few examples themselves indicate, either such principles have to be so general as to be quite ambiguous in application and therefore vacuous, or else they become so specific that they cannot be claimed to be the only possible Christian approach in every possible practical situation. The Churches should beware of issuing directives as if they have the unique authority of Christian scripture and tradition, when they are often only too clearly products of the specific social and geographical situation in which some Christians find themselves, and when Christians speaking from different points of view might just as conscientiously dissent from them. Deep ideological and social differences between Christians sometimes occur and are painful, but they must be faced and not hidden. The restatement of relevant theological themes that we have undertaken here is therefore not intended to yield generally applicable principles, but rather to encourage direct confrontation between theologians and technical specialists.

Our brief lies in the field of theology, and we offer this report as a group working in connection with the Church of England's Commission on Christian Doctrine. Because we are convinced that Christian theology can provide a unifying vision which we believe society must recover if attitudes are to change, it follows that theologians should meet with others to share and discuss problems concerning the environmental crisis. Such dialogue is mutually stimulating. Indeed, we are reminded that

this very report had its origins in a meeting between environmentalists and theologians. Our argument therefore forces us to
urge the pressing importance of inter-disciplinary discussions,
in which theologians will join with moral philosophers,
economists, agriculturalists, environmentalists, industrialists,
sociologists, politicians, and others. Such attitudes should show
how changed attitudes could result in changed policies at
regional, national and international levels. We hope that the
Churches will urgently promote such discussions on an ecumenical and open basis. We believe that the theological affirmations which we have outlined above and the attitudes which
flow from them are far from being matters of merely abstract
theology. They need urgently to be translated into terms of
contemporary political and economic programmes.[6] Both
nationally and internationally people yearn for social justice,
but the yearning is vain unless it is accompanied by changed
attitudes of openness and benevolence. No less does the whole
created order cry aloud for ecological harmony. But that cry
will remain unheeded unless there is a renewed vision, motiv-
ation and determination to make this world not only fit for
posterity to live in but also responsive to the aims and intentions of God who created it and who sanctifies it and who wills
to save it with the co-operation of mankind.

The future is unknown to us. We may be on the verge of a
new chapter of our civilization of which our present troubles
are only the growing pains, or we may be near the collapse of
modern culture through interior breakdown or through ecological disaster or the calamity of nuclear warfare. In an
essay later in the book, some possible futures of man are
sketched.[7] In the report itself we have been naturally concerned
with the present world situation in which we live. But we
must make clear, in conclusion, that the Christian faith is not

tied to any particular culture; and so it will continue to be relevant, whatever forms of culture and of society may emerge in the future. We wish to affirm that, whatever happens to modern civilization in this country and elsewhere – whether it collapses or renews itself – the Christian attitude to the future is characterized by hope, in the faith that God's purposes for his world will finally be fulfilled. Indeed, what might seem a disastrous setback can even, in the mercy of God, become a means of its fulfilment. So the Apostle Paul judged; and it led him to exclaim (Romans 11:33–6):

O the depth of the riches and wisdom and knowledge of God! How unsearchable are his judgements and how inscrutable his ways!
> 'For who has known the mind of the Lord,
>   or who has been his counsellor?'
> 'Or who has given a gift to him
>   that he might be repaid?'
For from him and through him and to him are all things. To him be glory for ever. Amen.

ESSAYS ON
MAN AND NATURE

BIBLICAL ATTITUDES TO NATURE

by John Austin Baker

The Old Testament

The writers of the Old Testament did not have, as we do, an immense stock of general or semi-abstract terms. While this limited them in some directions – the development of Hebrew philosophy and metaphysics, for example, had to wait for the enrichment of the language in post-biblical times – it also saved them from certain woollinesses of thought to which we are peculiarly liable. Thus, the lack of a word corresponding to our term 'nature' deprived them of a collective noun useful enough if carefully handled; but it also meant that they were safeguarded against lumping together things that have no obvious business together, and did not have (and so could not be taken in by) such phrases as 'communing with nature', or 'Nature, red in tooth and claw'. What they saw when they looked around them was not some undifferentiated global category, but concrete things – mountains, seas, rivers, crawling animals, oaktrees, birds, the sun and moon, and so on. Their nearest approach to an all-embracing word for their environment was 'the earth'.[1] The title 'Friends of the Earth' they would have understood. 'Nature-lover' would have required some explanation.

One result of these terminological differences is that we sometimes fail to recognize our own questions, and indeed our own answers to those questions, when they appear in the Old Testament in what we regard as 'less sophisticated' language. (It may not in fact be less sophisticated, only less imprecise.) Several such common areas of concern will emerge in the course of this essay. One in particular, however, will form a good starting-point for our discussion.

How far is man involved in nature, and how far has he distanced himself from it? Between them the Old Testament writers are aware of the basic elements of this question. Man is part of the panorama of nature. Psalm 104, for example, places him firmly, with great artistry, in the context of all the other teeming life of the earth. Nothing is done to highlight him; he is just another figure in the landscape:

> Thou makest darkness, and it is night,
>> when all the beasts of the forest creep forth.
> The young lions roar for their prey,
>> seeking their food from God.
> When the sun rises, they get them away
>> and lie down in their dens.
> Man goes forth to his work
>> and to his labour until the evening.
> O Lord, how manifold are thy works!
>> In wisdom hast thou made them all;
>> the earth is full of thy creatures (vv. 20-4).

By contrast, both the creation stories in Genesis, in their individual ways, stress the distinctness of man from the rest of creation, while in one of them his homogeneity with it is at least played down. In the older story (J), Genesis 2:4b-25, both man and the animals are formed out of the dust of the ground (vv. 7,19); but the birds and beasts are nevertheless not adequate companions and partners for man (v. 20). Only another human being, formed out of his own living substance, can be that (vv. 21–3). It is this unique kinship which, so the story claims, explains the all-surpassing force of the bond between man and woman (v. 24).

The superiority of man to the animals is further emphasized in this story by the incident of man's naming of all the living creatures. God brings the animals which he has created to man to see what will happen; and man expresses his innate superiority by giving them their names, names which from thenceforward are unalterably the ones that properly belong to them (vv. 19–20). This incident has two important implications. First, to give a name to some other being is to claim and exercise sovereignty over it. One obvious example is the authority of a parent over a newborn child; but the naming prerogative is also a mark of a political overlord (cf. 2 Kings 24:17). Similarly, the fact that Adam gives a name to his wife at her first creation (2:23) implies the male hegemony characteristic of the writer's own world, though this lordship is modified by the actual name chosen,[2] which emphasizes that woman is the only creature who belongs in the same category as man. After the expulsion from Eden, Adam exerts his authority over his wife once more by giving her a new name (3:20). So, the giving of names to the animals by man is a mark of legitimate supremacy over them; and it is by this act that man proves to God that none of God's new creatures is in fact a 'helper fit for him' (vv. 18,20). Secondly, there is the strong conviction of the whole ancient world, which the biblical writers shared, that a true name expresses the nature and controls the destiny of its owner (cf., for example, Genesis 35:16–18, the two names of Rachel's last child). By giving the animals the truly appropriate name for each Adam proves that he has insight into their true nature, that he understands them.

This at once puts him on a different plane from them; he is a creature nearer to God than they, and in fact sharing some at any rate of the insight that enabled God to create them in the first place. Man's natural role, therefore, is one of sovereignty over other creatures – not the absolute sovereignty that belongs to God alone, but at least a relative authority and superiority. That this is the correct reading of the story is confirmed by the form which man's own punishment for his disobedience takes in Genesis 3. Because he has rebelled against his proper over-lord, God, his own subjects are to rebel against him; and the ground which once he tilled with ease (2:15) now yields less, and even that only to unremitting labour (3:17–19).

In the later creation narrative (Genesis 1:1–2:4a) man's supremacy is spelt out categorically. His kinship with God is given technical theological expression: he is 'in [God's] image' and 'after [his] likeness' (Genesis 1:26–7). The exact meaning of this phrase has been endlessly debated. There may be influence from the Egyptian formula according to which the Pharaoh is 'the image of Amun-Re', in which case there are viceregal overtones, made explicit in verse 28. But the Hebrew and Egyptian phrases are not truly parallel. Much more certain is the implication that man is the nearest visible pointer to what God looks like (cf. Ezekiel 1:26). The interesting question is: how far is this similarity thought to go below the surface into the realm of understanding and moral character? To some degree it must do, since it is inherently improbable that any writer would make God give even a shadow of his own unique likeness to a creature that had nothing in common with him; and this common-sense conclusion is confirmed by the fact that God entrusts dominion over his new and wonderful earth and its inhabitants to man.

The major difference between this creation story and the older one, so far as our present subject is concerned, is that in Genesis 1, while the superiority of man to the rest of the animal world, though expressed in more explicit imagery, is probably no more radical than it is in Genesis 2,[3] the theme of a common physical origin for men and animals is suppressed altogether. The writer of Genesis 1 seems to have held a view, of which there are other instances in the ancient world, that the earth and the sea themselves 'brought forth' their various inhabitants (vv. 20-1, 24-5), but he has combined this with safeguards against any divinization of earth and sea by insisting simultaneously that in fact God himself 'created' (v. 21) and 'made' (v. 25) the creatures which these primordial entities generated. The resultant picture, then, is that all animal life was 'produced' either by the earth or by the sea, as a result of God's creative edict and operation. There is here a very careful gradation upwards from the production of plant life (vv. 11-12), where God issues the creative fiat, 'Let the earth put forth vegetation, etc.', but is not said to have 'made' or 'created' what is put forth. The writer seems to be saying that animal life, whether on land or in the sea, is more marvellous than mere plant life, and, although issuing from the womb of the earth and from the waters, required a special operation of God to bring it about. Now, in the case of man we take yet another step upwards. Here the divine edict and activity are everything: no intermediate creative source is named. Whereas in Genesis 2 both man and animals were fashioned by God from the soil, here man is presented as created[4] by God directly, and the question whether he too came from the earth is at least passed over in silence. It is possible that Psalm 139:15 draws on a myth that man was 'earth-born'. If such a view was current, then the writer of Genesis 1 has deliberately snubbed it; and this would

MAN AND NATURE

strengthen our impression that he is intentionally minimizing those features common to man and the animals.

Man in Genesis 1, indeed, occupies much the same high place in the scheme of things as he does in Psalm 8:

Yet thou hast made him little less than God,
   and dost crown him with glory and honour.
Thou hast given him dominion over the works of thy hands;
   thou hast put all things under his feet,
all sheep and oxen,
   and also the beasts of the field,
the birds of the air, and the fish of the sea,
   whatever passes along the paths of the sea (vv. 5–8).

To our ears such words sound very like the most blatant human imperialism *vis-à-vis* the rest of nature, as does the divine commission to man in Genesis 1:28; and in modern times they may have fostered and been used to justify such an attitude. But what in their biblical context did they originally imply?

It is highly probable that one connection of this type of language is with the institution of kingship. Under the influence of Mesopotamian models even quite petty kings in the ancient Near East seem to have used cosmic iconography to express their status and authority. Solomon's lion throne, with six steps and a curved back (1 Kings 10:18–20), as we know from archaeological parallels, symbolized world dominion; and the embroidery on the collar of the later high priests, which was probably zodiacal and signified the whole cosmos, was almost certainly taken over from the royal robes of earlier times (cf. Wisdom of Solomon 18:24a). 'Kingship came down from heaven', the ancient Near East believed; and part of the mystique of kingship was that every king was God's vicegerent on earth. Now, one of a king's most important duties was to ensure fertility and prosperity by his obedience to the gods and by his observance of the yearly rituals. We can trace thinking of this kind in the Old Testament, not only in such an incident as the famine sent on Israel for the wickedness of Ahab (1 Kings 17:1) but, more positively, in a text like Psalm 72, where unimaginable abundance is to be a mark of the reign of the ideal ruler. The conditions pictured in this psalm certainly never obtained at any historical epoch – the world-wide dominion described in verse 8, for example, was never actually attained even by those Mesopotamian overlords from whose honorifics the phrase in question was borrowed – but the psalm is nonetheless not just a dream of an indefinite future. Verse 1 refers to an actual king; it is a prayer, perhaps used at his coronation, that the vision painted in the psalm may come true in *this* king's reign. Primarily, therefore, the 'man' and 'son of man' of Psalm 8 is also the king, whose sacred office endows him with the resources of divine power not just over his human subjects but over all other creatures within his domain; and it is only his sins which cause this power to be withheld. Inevitably, therefore, as hopes pinned on human rulers are falsified, the vision of a world of abundance and peace becomes part of a hope set on God alone. In his own good time he will bring this to pass, and all the anomalies of both man and nature will be ironed out, and harmony will reign. Perhaps the most famous Old Testament instance of this eschatological hope for nature is Isaiah 11. But, by a well-known feature of human mythical thinking, paradise in the end-time is thought of as the re-creation of a primeval paradise at the dawn of creation, the lost 'golden age'. And that is how it comes about that in both the Old Testament creation stories we have the picture of man, the ideal king, God's perfect vicegerent, under whom nature is fertile and peaceful and all she was meant to be. A small but striking detail confirming this is the vegetarianism of the creation in Genesis 1: animals eat grass, man eats grains and fruits. It is no surprise, then, to find precisely this feature in Isaiah 11, the vision of paradise regained:

> The wolf shall dwell with the lamb,
>   and the leopard shall lie down with the kid,
> and the calf and the lion and the fatling together,
>   and a little child shall lead them.
> The cow and the bear shall feed;
>   their young shall lie down together;
>   and the lion shall eat straw like the ox . . .
> They shall not hurt or destroy
>   in all my holy mountain (vv. 6–7, 9a).

The 'dominion', therefore, which man is promised in Genesis 1 is poles apart from the kind of right to egotistical exploitation which it suggests to our ears. It is in essence a perfect obedience to the will of God which is rewarded by a divinely ordained harmony and abundance in nature, which recognizes man as the greatest of all God's creatures and pays him homage. If this vision offers any goals or ideals for our present situation, they certainly are not the extermination of species or the ruthless exploitation for short-term gain of precious natural resources. On the contrary, they are much more akin to the aims of modern study of animal life and of environmental conservation. Their relevance to technological questions can only be very indirect, worked out by applying the underlying theological attitudes in situations unimaginable to the original writers.

The Old Testament expresses in a number of ways the idea that man declined drastically from the standards of the golden age. The story of Cain and Abel (Genesis 4) is but the first and best known instance. Another, of more direct interest in our present context, is the change in the divine laws of life after the Flood. Mankind had become so corrupt that a cataclysmic destruction was the only remedy; the family of righteous Noah, eight persons only, are the sole survivors. This new start for the human race is marked by a divine covenant which, being modelled ultimately on the treaties imposed unilaterally in some ancient Near Eastern empires by suzerains on their vassals, contains both promises by the overlord and obligations laid upon his subjects. The promise is that never again will God destroy all living things (Genesis 9:8–17).[5] It is interesting and important that the covenant is made not just with man but also with all living creatures (five times repeated: vv. 10, 12, 15, 16, 17) and, indeed, with the earth itself (v. 13). The new laws of life (9:1–7) replace the ordinances established at the creation, and modify them in significant respects. No longer is man's food to be fruit and grain only: 'Every moving thing that lives shall be food for you; and as I gave you the green plants, I give you everything' (9:3). The Flood and the subsequent new start for the world are used as an opportunity to switch from the theoretic 'golden age' to the conditions actually obtaining;[6] and one of the saddest features of this change is the degradation of relations between man and the animals from their first created beauty. The language of Genesis 9:1–2, when compared with the same writer's phrasing in 1:28f., betrays at once the poignancy of his feelings:

> The fear of you and the dread of you shall be upon every beast of the earth, and upon every bird of the air, upon everything that creeps on the ground and all the fish of the sea; into your hand they are delivered (v. 2).

The language is that normally used of a conqueror slaughtering a routed army or sacking a fallen city. Man has become the enemy of all living things.[7]

The Old Testament, then, does nothing to justify the charge that it represents an exploitative, humanly egotistical attitude to nature. Although it recognizes man's preying on nature as a fact, it characterizes that fact as a mark of man's decline from the first perfect intentions of God for him. This is in tune with another notable feature of the Old Testament, namely that it is permeated with what we can only call an affectionate and admiring approach to nature. We have seen this already in Psalm 104, and it is to be found in other psalms which are not, as is Psalm 104, modelled on already existing foreign poetry.[8] It is particularly evident in the so-called 'wisdom literature',[9] with its many similes from observation of animals, weather, plant life, and so on. We also find a kindred spirit in some of the prophets, where the faithful obedience of non-human creatures to the divine will is contrasted with the faithlessness and perversity of men:

> Even the stork in the heavens
>   knows her times;
> and the turtledove, swallow, and crane
>   'keep the time of their coming;
> but my people know not
>   the ordinance of the Lord (Jeremiah 8:7).

This admiration of nature finds its climax in the book of Job, where the wonders of the natural order are used for a didactic purpose unique in the Bible, and possibly in all ancient literature: namely, to make the point that man's whole attitude to what goes on in the created order is wrong, because it is totally egoistic, totally anthropocentric. If he were to stop for even a moment to consider the universe as it actually is, he would see that by far the greater part of it has no relevance to him at all. If God created Behemoth and Leviathan, it assuredly was not for man's benefit (chs. 40–1); it must have been for some purpose opaque to man, who can think only in terms of himself and his situation. Such creatures glorify God in their existence according to rules far beyond our ken; he made them and delights in them for their own sake, not for some ulterior usefulness to us human beings. The same point is made in a rather different way by drawing Job's attention to the seemingly idiotic behaviour of certain animals such as the ostrich (39: 13–18), or to the apparent pointlessness of certain phenomena, such as the brief spring rains which cause a short-lived carpet of tiny flowers to appear in the desert (38:26–7). Why have flowers where there is no one to admire them? Man did not arrange any of these things; and if it had been left to him, he never would have done! But God did arrange them. We are left to draw our own conclusions: either that God is daft, or perhaps that we with our purely human-conditioned 'wisdom' take far too narrow and short-sighted a view ever to reach any genuine understanding of reality.

This is not to say that a sound and sensible way of dealing with nature is not a part of the wisdom appropriate to man, and as such itself a gift of God (cf. Isaiah 28:23–9). Not only is this accepted; it is in fact one particular application of a more general principle developed in the Old Testament, which is of some importance for our present subject. This is the principle that by observation of the way in which nature functions we can arrive at *moral* guidance for human life. In the Old Testament this is not taken beyond the most obvious instances: for example, the world is made in such a way that the lazy are likely to starve, and therefore it is wrong to be lazy. But significantly, such conduct is held to be wrong not just in a pragmatic sense but also in a theological one. For, as with everything else in the Old Testament, such thinking has an extra dimension, the omnipresent, omnirelevant fact of God. Since it was the wisdom of God which made the world, he must have had some purpose in every detail of its ordering, and he must, therefore, have intended laziness to be dangerous. Hence diligent and sensible work can be said to be something which God himself both commands and commends, and sloth something he condemns. There are, then, in the Old Testament elements to justify a pragmatic, science-based ethic, at least in some such general terms as these: that what by observation we discover really to work best, both for man and for other creatures, is something which loyalty to God requires us to put into practice. Even the 'extra' point about what is best for other creatures, which may seem very modern, is not without foundation in such a saying as this from Proverbs: 'A righteous man has regard for the life of his beast' (12:10) – where, be it noted, the quality that makes a man considerate of his working animals is not prudence or good business sense but 'righteousness', being fair.[10]

One reason why the Old Testament attitude to nature is more sympathetic and comprehensible to us than that of some other ancient Near Eastern peoples is that for a good many of the Old Testament writers, though not all, nature has been, to use a modern term, substantially 'demythologized'. An example may clarify the point. In the Ugaritic texts of the mid-second millennium occurs the following passage:

> If thou smite Lotan, the serpent slant,
>   Destroy the serpent tortuous,
> Shalyat of the seven heads . . .

The name Lotan is generally agreed to be the Canaanite

equivalent of one which appears many centuries later in the Old Testament, and to which we have already referred, namely, Leviathan, who is also a sea-monster. In the Old Testament Leviathan plays a number of roles. In Psalm 74 he is, as in Ugarit, many-headed, and also an enemy of God.[11] In Isaiah 27:1 we have mention of 'Leviathan the fleeing serpent, Leviathan the twisting serpent', another very close parallel to the Ugaritic text; but here the monster symbolizes cosmic evil, to be overthrown by God at the Last Day. In striking contrast to both these uses of the Leviathan figure, however, are Psalm 104 and Job 41. In Psalm 104 Leviathan is a pet, with whom God enjoys playing in his leisure moments (v. 26); and in the second he is the greatest of all God's creatures, 'king over all the sons of pride', and is cited simply to crush the anthropocentric conceit of Job. If we try to date these passages, we find no steady theological trend. A majority vote of scholarly opinion would probably give the sequence: Psalm 104 – Psalm 74 – Isaiah 51 – Job 41 – Isaiah 27. In other words, running side by side we have the sea as something evil and as something good, and the monster as a symbol of anti-God forces and as a magnificent testimony to God's wisdom and glory and power.

The theological background to this ongoing activity of 'demythologizing' which developed in certain quarters in Israel may be analysed, very crudely and briefly, as follows. The basic premise of Israel's faith is that her God is stronger than anything or anyone. And whether or not she worked this out by precise logical argumentation, Israel found herself driven in the end to the conclusion that, for this to be so, God had to be radically distanced from natural phenomena. Other nations had advanced, it is true, well beyond the stage of a simple-minded identification of gods with natural forces or objects; but they were trapped in the morass of polytheism, and one of the reasons for this was that the traditional associations of various deities with particular phenomena – the sun, the moon, the stars, storms, vegetation, the sea, and so on – meant that the obvious multiplicity of nature kept getting in the way of their struggles to apprehend the unity of the divine. Thought and language very different from those of the ancient Semitic world were needed before metaphysical speculation enabled men to punch their way out of that bag. But by a kind of inspired bigotry the Jews succeeded where others failed. By sticking doggedly to the one thesis that 'my God can lick your god any day', they found themselves forced to treat everything as subordinate to Yahweh, indeed as his instrument:

> who makest the winds thy messengers,
> fire and flame thy ministers (Psalm 104:4).

The Old Testament nowhere offers a positive definition of God's nature, to say how he differs from all other beings. It simply implies that he does by proclaiming that they all without exception do as he tells them. And this has two very important consequences for the Old Testament attitude to nature. First, nature is progressively depersonalized and demythologized. It is no longer the manifestation of supernatural beings, but now for the first time actually merits the name 'nature' – though, of course, the Hebrew language did not have that name available to use. The climax of this process in the Old Testament is to be found in the book of Ecclesiastes, which in many ways needs no updating whatever to be fully acceptable to our own outlooks on the world.[12] A 'natural' interpretation of nature makes its first appearance on the human scene in the Old Testament. Secondly, following on from this, man loses his numinous dread of nature. Nature can still frighten him, but only by virtue of being stronger than he in a natural way, from which he may need God to rescue him, but which he recognizes now as being in principle a strength he can understand and in many cases do something about.

We may, then, summarize the main points emerging from the Old Testament utterances about nature as follows:

1. For the Old Testament writers the determining factors in thinking about nature, as on every other subject, are the all-controlling rights and power of God. 'The earth is the Lord's and the fullness thereof' (Psalm 24:1); and this can be carried so far even as to have practical consequences for human social legislation, as in the principles underlying the law of Jubilee, that no human being can ever 'own' land, but must be regarded as a tenant installed by God (Leviticus 25:1-34). Since God is thought of as having a moral and rational character, man must in the end submit to 'things as they are' as the revelation of that goodness and wisdom; or, in our terms, he must ultimately be controlled by respect for the intricate character and needs of the natural order, and cannot violate it by his technology for his own ends without expecting at least long-term retribution.

2. Within this overall condition man does have a position of control over nature, which is approved by God; but the tyrannical use of this position is a failure deriving from human sin, not from God's intention in creation.

3. Man's proper control is made possible because the realization that God is One and transcendent effectively de-supernaturalizes the world, ridding it of superhuman personal power, whether divine or demonic, and placing man in a position to use his powers rationally in dealing with nature.

4. Nevertheless, nature is not to be evaluated simply in terms of man's needs and interests; and to think that it is, is merely a mark of folly. God created the greater part of the world for

its own sake; and wisdom consists in recognizing this, and the limitations which this imposes on us, so that the truly 'wise' man will never imagine that he knows fully what God was 'at' in creation.

5. The wise and comprehensive observation of nature will, however, yield indications for human behaviour which were part of God's intention in creating in the first place, and which therefore have the status of moral imperatives for man.

The New Testament

By contrast with the Old Testament the New Testament has relatively little to say about man's proper attitude to nature. The reasons for this are some fortuitous, some perhaps socio-logical, but some inherent in the nature of the primitive Christian community and its world-view.

The fortuitous reasons arise purely from the scale and character of the New Testament material. The volume of the New Testament, to start with, is only 30 per cent of that of the Old. The bulk of its contents fall within a period of forty years, and the outside limits of its dating bracket less than a century, compared with the nine centuries lying between the earliest and latest passages in the Old Testament. The New Testament is the work of a relatively small, specialized community, whereas the Old Testament is the product of a whole nation, a minor one certainly, but always much larger than the Church in the New Testament period, and inevitably concerned with a wider variety of issues and situations. Consequently it is no surprise to find in the Old Testament far greater diversity of types of literature than in the New Testament. There is nothing in the New Testament, for example, to parallel the large collections of 'observations on life and world-order' which we call the wisdom literature of the Old Testament, or its extensive range of liturgical poetry, or the detailed corpus of its laws on what we would regard as secular matters. Hence the very types of material in which an attitude to nature might be most likely to be reflected are precisely those which are missing from the New Testament.

Sociologically, it is hard to escape the impression that most of the New Testament writers are 'urbanized', compared with the predominantly agricultural orientation of the mind of the Old Testament. The Gospel material, especially in the teaching of Jesus with its plentiful use of images from nature and husbandry, is nearest to the original Palestinian background, and so to the world of the Old Testament itself. But otherwise there is little sign in the writers of interest in nature as such; and their audiences, where known, are almost exclusively urban.

Nevertheless, when all this is said, there were yet other reasons, inherent in the earliest Church and its gospel, which conspired to minimize concern with the whole question of an attitude to nature. The first was the approach of primitive Christianity to scripture. For Christians of the first century the Old Testament was their Bible; it, and it alone, was the inspired word of God. It might be thought that this would awaken some interest at least in all the various subjects with which the Old Testament deals; but one overriding factor prevented this. Primarily and overwhelmingly the first Christians were interested in the Old Testament as a vast source-book of predictions, some clear, some enigmatic, of the coming of Christ, his nature, life, death, resurrection, redeeming work, and heavenly glory, and of the mission and destiny of the Church. The literal sense of a passage was, in most cases, of very much less importance than its prophetic meaning, which had to be disentangled by the use of allegorical exegesis, a device used by Christians, Jews and Gentiles alike on ancient and sacred texts. Nor were the readers of such texts particularly interested in the whole range of an argument, or the overall message of a book; these are characteristically modern ways of using scripture. For them, any verse, sentence or phrase could be taken, out of context if need be, and its reference to Christ extracted by what seems to us at times over-ingenious exposition, but which was simply something that sprang naturally, given the thought-forms of the day, from their exuberant and untiring obsession with the Gospel. Given this, it can be seen that those elements in Judaism which we have been considering in this essay were effectively blanked off from early Christian consciousness.

Secondly, there is the fact that the Christian message was initially a gospel of personal salvation. Certainly it impinged on ordinary life, but only at the points of religious belief and personal morality.[13] The members of the Church of Corinth received much instruction from St Paul, but none of it was directed at the matters we are considering. Indeed, when the Apostle does happen to mention a relevant Old Testament text – 'You shall not muzzle an ox when it treads out the grain' (Deuteronomy 25:4) – he does so simply to apply it by the kind of allegorical interpretation we have just mentioned to the economic support of those who preach the Gospel. No doubt St Paul was not anti-oxen, but he is quite certain that God would not waste valuable inspired wordage on such a subject: 'Is it for oxen that God is concerned? Does he not speak entirely for our sake?' (1 Corinthians 9:10)

The third and perhaps the most important of all reasons is, of course, that the earliest Christians felt themselves to be those 'upon whom the end of the ages has come' (1 Corinthians 10:11). The 'form of this world' was passing away, the new age was about to dawn; and it was a serious question what would happen to the bodies of those who had not yet died when the Last Day came, and so could hardly be resurrected (1 Corinthians 15:51). The created order did not have long to run; and so there was no incentive to develop a constructive long-term attitude to nature as it was. It is in their successors of the second generation that we have to look for most of what modest amount the New Testament Church does have to say on this issue.

Turning now to this positive side, we note first that in the main, as its underlying tonality, so to speak, the New Testament adopts the basic attitude of the Old Testament, that the created order is God's work and as such is good. In the gospels, God's providential care extends even to the most insignificant animals, and the beauty of the wild flowers springing up in the fields of Galilee is greater than that of Solomon in all his glory (Matthew 6:26 = Luke 12:24; Matthew 10:29 = Luke 12:6; Matthew 6:28f.). There is no food which is unclean; impurity is a moral quality (Mark 7:19). In his parables Jesus encourages care and concern for animals (cf. Luke 13:15; 15:4; Matthew 12:11 = Luke 14:5), even if these are only illustrations incidental to his main point. In St Paul, the wonders of the creation are sufficient in themselves to lead the open and rational mind to God (Romans 1:20). He accepts, despite his rigorous Jewish upbringing, the liberating insight of Jesus that nothing is in itself unclean (Romans 14:14); and in discussing the question of meat offered to idols, while respecting the tender consciences of the more scrupulous brethren, he makes it clear that for himself, with his robust Jewish monotheism, reinforced by the revelation of God in Christ (1 Corinthians 8:4–6), there can be no problem, for 'the earth is the Lord's, and everything in it' (1 Corinthians 10:26,28). This fundamentally affirmative and confident attitude to the creation is reinforced by the doctrine of *creatio ex nihilo* (Hebrews 11:3), which, as we noted, was not available to the Old Testament writers, emerging as it does in the inter-testamental period. And in a later work, the Acts of the Apostles, there are signs of a very positive theology of the natural order developing with the assimilation of the Middle Platonist thought of Hellenistic Judaism (Acts 17:24–8).

Nevertheless, even though the basic tonality, to pursue our metaphor, is in character that of the major key, it is shadowed from time to time by more sombre material in the minor. This is a reflection of the pessimism and anxiety afflicting the Mediterranean world around the turn of the eras. In Judaism it found expression in that apocalyptic despair which in certain circles regarded the whole of the present created order as beyond redemption, and looked for a cataclysmic irruption of God to establish a new order from which evil would be banished. The wide dissemination in the Near and Middle East at this time of dualistic faiths, the staple of that religious phenomenon loosely labelled 'Gnosticism', was another manifestation of the same *malaise*; while in Hellenism many suffered from a 'sense of helplessness in the hands of fate', which made them 'wonder whether it is possible to be at home in the world at all'. Because the world had become 'a hostile, alien place', they turned to astral cults. 'The lower world was not centred in itself, but was under the control of the stars . . . Hence, in the last resort all activity here is trivial and meaningless, and if it seems to be independent, that is a mere illusion.'[14]

These contemporary trends are reflected in the New Testament. Partly their influence is seen in vigorous reaction against such beliefs, not by denying the reality to which they referred, but by claiming that in the Gospel men were delivered from helpless subjection to that reality. Thus, in such passages as Galatians 4:3, Colossians 2:8,15, and Ephesians 6:12, the Christian is exhorted to enter into the freedom Christ has won for him, and to fight against the domination of the hypercosmic powers. Again, in Romans 8:9-22, Paul accepts the truth in the Jewish apocalyptic view that the world is in 'bondage to decay', and that the whole creation 'groans in travail'; but he places this in a transformed theological perspective by insisting that it is God who placed the creation in this bondage, and that its deliverance is to be brought about when the true children of God, those who have the Spirit of Jesus, are complete. Nevertheless, it is clear that the general diagnosis of the cosmic situation is not very different from that made by many other sects and schools of thought at the time. The Pauline tradition does not say, 'This is rubbish! All this talk of deep-seated corruption and bondage to Fate throughout the created order is nonsense.' On the contrary, it is taken very seriously; all that Christianity claims is that it has a better answer to the problem. And that answer, significantly enough, is not a means of redeeming the world of nature as well as the soul of man, so that they can then live in harmony to create the Kingdom of God on earth, but a spiritual liberation of those men and women who believe in Jesus, who must then wait in patience for a total remaking of the cosmos in God's own time, and by God's own hand. The book of Revelation, with its vision of a new heaven and a new earth (Revelation 21:1), is the logical culmination of this approach.

As time went on, a more optimistic note becomes discernible, chiefly in opposition to the false asceticism characteristic of the dualistic sects. Thus, 1 Timothy 4:3-4 commends the right use

of God's gifts in the order of creation. And there was one theological concept in particular in the later New Testament writings which offered a theoretical foundation for this more
affirmative attitude. This was the idea of the 'cosmic Christ'.
In various forms the conception is developed that the pre-
existent divine Christ was himself the divine agent in creation,
and that the existence of all things is in some way upheld by
him. We find this in such diverse writings as Hebrews (1:3)
and Colossians (1:16f.); but most notably in the prologue to
the fourth gospel (John 1:1-4). The implications of this idea for
a theology of nature are not, of course, worked out in the New
Testament itself; but, obscure as the thought-forms undoubtedly
are to us, there does shine through them a conviction that the
whole universe, could we but see it, is in its essential nature in
harmony not merely with some unknown divine power but
with God as revealed in Jesus, and that therefore there must be
some *modus vivendi* between man and nature which is in
keeping with all that is best in both.

Conclusion

In seeking for any kind of theology of man and nature, the
Christian cannot but be grateful that his Bible does not consist
merely of the New Testament. Even the final point just mentioned, that of the 'cosmic Christ', would be virtually unusable
were it not built on the world-affirming monotheism of the
Old Testament, which can proclaim that God 'saw everything
that he had made, and behold, it was very good'. Perhaps
there is no field of thought in which the classic Christian view
of redemption and revelation is so palpably justified as in this.
. For it must be clear from what has been said in this brief

summary of the biblical materials relevant to our subject that the best hope for a constructive religious approach to the urgent practical problems of our day can arise only out of that whole strand in human history constituted by Israel and the Church together, working with all those who in various creeds and philosophies have drawn on that tradition, and not out of those elements in the whole which are specific to the purely Christian gospel.

NATURAL EVIL

by Don Cupitt

Since the report deals with the great issues of God's relation to nature, and his purpose in raising up man out of nature, we cannot avoid confronting the problem of evil. For man is a worker, who transforms nature by his labour; so that the differing views about technology current today rest in the end on different views about what, if anything, is wrong with nature, and to what end it should be modified by human work.

Let me make this clear by sketching two contrary views. Suppose first that we envisage nature as a kindly mother, lovely in every aspect. In that case we should say that man's life and work ought to run in harmony with her, trusting in her wisdom. Our educational practice would rely on the child's innate aptitudes and its desire to learn. Our ethic would be an ethic of spontaneous natural feeling, with little emphasis upon original sin. Our farming and our technology would be cyclical and 'organic', following the circular movements of water, carbon, nitrogen and so on in nature, and tapping the energy of wind, sun and water. Our gardening would be 'natural' in the later eighteenth-century manner, rather than formal in the earlier fashion. We would be enthusiastic for breast-feeding, and for the preventive medicine and dentistry which work by strengthening the body's natural defences.

Alternatively, suppose we take a pessimistic view of nature, seeing her as wild, chaotic and pitiless. Our culture would, in that case, be a culture of reason, will and order. Human life and work would be seen as a disciplined effort to overcome and contain nature's disorderly unreliability. Art would celebrate a formal ideal of order, rather than merely copy nature. Our horticulture and our educational theory alike would aim to discipline wild nature. Our ethics would express the triumph of will over unruly natural impulse. Our technology would be deliberately contra-natural, the construction of a friendly artificial environment to defend us against nature's violence. We might well be enthusiastic for bottle-feeding, high-technology medicine and dentistry, strict sexual morals and strong government.

These are broad sketches of two extremes, and I do not suggest that people are ever entirely consistent in their attitudes. Nevertheless, I do suggest that we have here two roughly co-herent clusters of opinions, both of which have a long history in our tradition.

The first group, today's progressives, are the environmental-ists. I would expect to find among them a good many feminists, and few believers in original sin. I would expect them to be-lieve in the primacy of feeling, of biology rather than engineer-ing, and in fresh food rather than processed food; and that in education they would look for something more like an English primary school than a French *lycée*.

The second group, today's conservatives, have a more 'Augustinian-Puritan' attitude to nature. Their outlook is masculine: they believe in the will and in the machine; in physics, engineering and technology. As reason should rule the passions so (the symbolism suggests), man should rule nature, harnessing her, exploiting her, and making a comfortable home for himself out of her. This group appeals to tradition, to the achievements of the last century or so, and concludes that technological problems can only be solved by more technology.

The will to mastery must simply affirm itself more strongly, and not falter at the first sign of difficulty.

Cardinal Manning said once that all problems are ultimately theological. On this occasion, he was right: our attitudes to questions as diverse as the theory of dentistry, the practice of gardening and the emancipation of women all ultimately depend upon how we characterize nature, man's place in nature, and the relation of nature and man to God.

So now to evil, and in particular to the question of natural evil.

The classical writers on the problem of evil, who flourished around the time of Newton, divided all evils into three kinds: metaphysical, natural and moral.[1]

Metaphysical evil was supposed to comprise the imperfections or limitations which must exist in any created world at all. Any created world, it was claimed, must be less perfect than the creator. For any created world, it would be best that it should be plural, to allow variety; and changing, to allow development. It would be best that the many creatures should all be different from each other, to make up a various and interdependent whole; and that changes should be governed by laws, so that they may be intelligible. Rationality, given that it is good, demands an orderly world to be known. So in one way and another a large number of the most general ills of life were explained as necessary constituents of any worthwhile created world at all.

Moral evils were described as all those evils which are the direct consequence of human misdeeds. Here the 'free-will defence' was invoked. A world in which creatures are free to choose evil (and, be it noted, actually do choose it, and by their choice bring evil upon their own *and* others' heads) is better than a world without free choice.

Natural evils remained between these two categories. They were all those evils (things or events of which one can rightly say that they ought not to have existed or occurred) which take place apart from human choice, and yet do not seem to be inevitable or necessary constituents of the world-process. Various examples are given: in physical nature, violent catastrophes such as volcanic eruptions, earthquakes and great storms; in organic nature, predation, parasitism, competition and animal pain in general; and in human life, still-births, untimely death, deformity, lingering disease, madness and the rest of the long tale of human suffering. Natural evils are those ills which lead us most seriously to question the justice of God.

This distinction of evil into three kinds clearly has a great deal wrong with it, for one can cite all manner of examples which cut across it. Take death, for example. It might be regarded as a metaphysical evil, for some bold philosopher might argue that if any created world ought to be plural and changing, then it must contain generation and corruption. But for a long time death was regarded as a moral evil, a punishment for human sin. More recently it has been regarded as a natural evil. Yet others again, remembering Tithonus and Swift's Struldbrugs, who were cursed with earthly immortality, might say that to the wise man death is not an evil at all, but 'of all sleeps the sweetest'. The book of Genesis itself, still our basic myth, alternates between treating death as a punishment, and seeing it as being the proper consummation of life, beautiful as harvest and sunset.[2]

So it is far from agreed whether death as such is an evil at all, still less what kind of evil it is. Many have said the same about animal pain. The layman, seeing the life of insects or of the seashore in close-up for the first time, may recoil in horror;

but the trained biologist comes to see things differently. It is not that he becomes stony-hearted or amoral in his outlook, but rather that as he learns to look at living things in a truly biological way, as he learns more about adaptation, and ecology, and the interdependence of all life in its habitat, he learns to look at the phenomena less anthropomorphically, and to accept the living world as a whole. The humblest bug is more complex, more exquisitely adapted to its mode of being, than the most advanced airliner. The intricacy and the fierce battle for living space, the beauty and the cruelty, come to seem parts of an indissoluble whole. There is in insects particularly, perhaps, the overall impression of an unquenchable vitality and resourcefulness, an indomitable striving, such as is occasionally met in great artists, and leads us to call their genius 'a force of nature'. It may indeed be premoral, but it is admirable nonetheless: it is magnificence. For a Christian, it should not be worshipped, but it should certainly be revered, and it is all about us, in the two-year-old child, in the house-fly buzzing round the lampshade, in the spider behind the sink.

Again, and before we digress further, natural evil and moral evil are intertwined. Men go on living in places where earthquakes are known to be probable. When one occurs, and they are killed, do we blame them or God?

So the lines between the different kinds of evil are blurred; and it is often unclear what is to be reckoned evil. But we can, I believe, make some use of modern knowledge to amend the terms of the older debates.

In the first place, the *corruptibility* of nature was, in antiquity, often supposed to be a sign that something was wrong with it. The sublunary world of change and decay was contrasted unfavourably with the changeless perfection of the heavens. Galileo put an end to this contrast between the terrestrial and celestial worlds. Even stars, we now say, are born and die, and corruption is an essential part of the world-process, for it is *renewal*. In the past men made things to be as durable as possible; but recently we have begun consciously to manufacture degradable commodities. To say that plastics which rot are better is to evince a new attitude to corruption.

But secondly, we have learned to look historically at nature, and the emergence of man from nature. This change alters our whole idea, not only of the relation of man *to* nature, but also of the divine purpose *for* man *in* nature. And it suggests a complex but important analogy between man, nature and our idea of God. These things are all built up from below.

God has built up the universe from below. He did not start by creating seraphim, and then work downwards, as men used to think. He started with raw energy. Out of it there gradually evolved the hundred chemical elements: from them emerged organic molecules: from them, living things: and from them, mankind. Our picture nowadays is historical, but the stages we place earlier in the story have not disappeared, but are still operative. Nature is built up from below, and physics remains yet the fundamental science of nature.

Man, too, is built up from below, not only in the historical sense, but in the structure of his personality. Freud, above all, understood this and his fundamental insight here is sound. From the infant's innocently egotistical biological drives, by a complex process of transformation and elaboration, adult personality develops. The loftiest genius, the noblest passion, are built from the humblest biological bricks. Freud's myth is, admittedly, a myth; but an illuminating myth. And post-Freudian worries about whether 'pure' human goodness is possible (because disinterested conduct has to be constructed out of selfish bricks) are analogous to modern worries about the emergence of natural beauty from a cruelly competitive process.

And similarly with our idea of God. Modern religious thought tends to work with the idea of a God who is infinite, perfect, purely rational and benevolent; forgetting that a very different deity rampages through documents still regarded as canonical. The God of modern piety himself evolved from a fearsome and capricious tribal deity, jealous of his own honour, uncompromising in his loves and hates, fiercely demanding, and capable of savagery. I am speaking psychologically, of course, of the idea of God which was in the minds of the men who wrote the earliest parts of the Hebrew Bible; but my point is this – modern consciousness is historical, and our thought of God must be so too. I am not talking about God in himself, but about the idea of God with which we have in practice to operate: an idea which reflects the ambiguities of nature and of man, and with respect to which in each case we have nowadays to accept that perfect beauty is made from humble elements through a long hard struggle. Scripture itself says that the goodness and justice of God will only become unambiguously manifest at the end of time, when his purpose for man and nature is complete.

The Christian and Jewish idea of God is derived from an historical revelation. It is the product of, and it reflects, the historical development of mankind through various stages of culture – tribal, national, and international; nomadic, agricultural, and urban. Our idea of God, based on revelation, has an historical dimension, as the Church affirms by continuing to use in worship passages from Genesis and Judges, as well as from 1 Corinthians and 1 John.

The analogy I have drawn suggests that as the laws of physics still underlie the movement of Rembrandt's brush;

and as the baby's cry for the breast is still present in the prayer of St John of the Cross; so the tribal God of the ancient Hebrews is still present in the God of St John's gospel. I am drawing an analogy between the way we see nature historically, the way we see the self historically, and the way in which *revelation itself* directs us to God historically; and then applying this complex analogy to the problem of evil.

To avoid misunderstanding, it ought to be added that the 'historical' consciousness in question here is that of Sigmund Freud and Claude Lévi-Strauss, not that of a nineteenth-century historicist. The 'historical' is the primeval, fundamental structure of the presently-experienced object. And I use the phrase 'our idea of God', rather than simply 'God', by way of stressing that, having no direct apprehension of him, we are dependent, even in revelation itself, upon historically conditioned imagery for our concrete idea of God.

There is, then, an analogy here. I look at the Small Tortoise-shell butterfly on the *Buddleia* in the garden. Absorbed in drinking, it allows me within a foot's distance. Every detail of its structure, and its life-history, is of amazing beauty. But I think too of the parasitic ichneumon, and of the evolutionary theory through which, nowadays, we cannot but look at any living thing. I am willing to accept the package as a whole, generation and corruption, beauty and transience and harshness. I'd better: there's no more to say. And if I accept *that*, then I also accept something analogous about human nature, about myself, about life; and even, in a sense, about the God of nature.

But now we have returned to the biologist's satisfaction in studying the premoral magnificence of wild nature; and we have to build something more specifically Christian upon it; for we must say that by itself that satisfaction is not enough.

There is a mood about today which says that wild nature is
so much more splendid than the products of human work, and
the impact of man upon nature is becoming such an immense
disaster, that man himself increasingly looks like a cancerous
growth upon our blue and white globe. One can see the be-
ginnings of despair about man's impact on nature; and one
can see the reasons for this despair. Think how beautiful the
Mediterranean world was in classical antiquity, and even until
1850. There was hardship, suffering and injustice aplenty; but
the land, the sea, and the works of man were fair; whereas now
the seas Odysseus sailed are beginning to die and the beaches
are fouled. I once saw by moonlight the coast where Aphrodite
was begotten and stepped ashore: what will it be when the
tourist industry has finished with it?

The temptation to pessimism is very strong; and it may lead
us to hate man and all his works, and fall into a pagan romanti-
cization of wild nature. Christians must find courage to affirm
that wild nature is not enough, because it is prehuman and
premoral. Through man's work the wilderness is to be made
a garden, the animal kingdom to come to praise its maker, and
raw minerals, the products of volcanoes, earthquakes and
sedimentation, to be made into great sculpture and buildings.
God through Christ redeems human nature in man himself;
and through his work man extends redemption to wild nature.
It is a crazily ambitious dream, horribly at variance with what
men are doing at present, but we dare affirm it possible, because here and there, on a small scale, it has been done. Through
his work man can perfect nature: actually improve upon it.
Nothing could be less true than the cliché that we live in an
age of optimistic secular humanism, whose confidence
Christians ought to try to sap. The opposite is nearer the
case. Modern men have largely lost confidence in themselves

and their work; and Christians ought to try to restore it by every means possible. For ever since Imhotep, the first known architect, there has perhaps never been a time when men so despaired of their ability to create a great monument, a fine city, as they do today. The performance in practice of the capitalist and communist systems makes many sceptical about the prospects of making even a just society. Many Christians nowadays are rightly sympathetic to the conservationist/ ecological movement; but we cannot accept the extreme pessimism about man and his work implicit in some of what it says and does, because the Gospel will not let us. The Gospel says that man is not a blight on nature, but crowns her; that God is not the God of the past, but of the future; and that through the incarnation of God in man redemption avails for man himself, and through man's God-inspired work, for nature. Though the outlook is not bright at the moment, we must not accept that nothing as good as Venice in her heyday will ever be made again.

We have discussed the question of natural evil, and have been led to a rather paradoxical conclusion. We live in an age undistinguished by any remarkable achievements in religion or art. Our one great distinction is in our highly-developed sciences of nature. We are very good at describing and explaining what is; but less good in grasping what ought to be and be done. We are even losing confidence in our technology.

So today men are more likely to admire wild nature's fast-vanishing splendour than to complain of her defects. They lack confidence that they can improve upon and adorn nature, for they lack the inspiration in morals, art and religion which might make their work sublime. Men are today transforming the world more and more rapidly, with worse and worse results, and they know it.

The Christian respects wild nature, but neither regards it as an end in itself, nor worships it. It is not yet perfected, but waits for its redemption, which will come through the work of men redeemed by God in Christ. That God is enigmatic in nature is no more surprising than that he is so in Genesis: all he is, all he can do, will not be manifest until the end of all things.

ON THE ALLEGED
INCOMPATIBILITY BETWEEN
CHRISTIANITY AND SCIENCE

by Mary Hesse

Scientific theories are attempts to interpret and explain experimental data by giving a unified picture of matter and its processes. (I shall restrict the discussion here to *natural* as opposed to social science.) Fundamental theories often make use of *models*, that is, they compare the ultimate building blocks and structures of the world with more familiar events such as mechanisms, or fluid vortices, or wave-motions. But such models are never finally proved by the data; they are always tentative and incomplete. In the past claims have sometimes been made that science can 'show' certain models of the world to be true, but recently philosophers of science have come to see more clearly that the history of science consists of sequences of such models (or 'paradigms', as Thomas Kuhn calls them[1]), each of which serve for a time, but are then superseded by quite different paradigms in what Kuhn describes as a 'revolutionary' manner.

In spite of lively controversy about the details of Kuhn's views, it would now be generally agreed by philosophers of science and by most scientists that the old picture of science as a continually progressive and accumulating sequence of discoveries about the inner nature of things is false. Of course, the *applications* of science accumulate, and provide possibilities of greater technical control over the world, and in this sense we learn more and more about how the world works, but this is a pragmatic rather than a theoretical type of knowledge. About the hidden structure of the world and its laws, we can do no better than propose a sequence of models, all of which turn out inadequate in the light of future research, and are replaced by others, sometimes by others that are radically different.

This account of scientific theories raises two important questions about the relation of science to theology, and in particular Christian theology. First, can scientific knowledge ever contradict or disprove Christian doctrine? And second, since scientific theory itself cannot be wholly derived from experimental data, where do its models or paradigms come from? In the science of the past they quite clearly came partly from theological and philosophical beliefs. This suggests that scientific theory and religion may sometimes attain a synthesis, and in any case it suggests that when there are disputes, these will be about philosophical assumptions and not about scientific facts. The distinction between theories and facts is important, for theologies and ideologies have often made themselves ridiculous by persisting in beliefs that are clearly contradicted by scientific discoveries of the sort which must, as far as we can see, be accommodated by any adequate theory. It is, for example, a fact that the universe is much older than six thousand years, and it is a fact (this time one frequently disbelieved by Marxist theorists) that the great majority of inheritable modifications in men's biological make-up take place by chance mutations of genes, and not by environmental conditioning.

But apparent contradictions between deep scientific theories and ideological beliefs are never so clear-cut. Looking back on two of the classic disputes of the 'science-religion conflict' we can now see that both sides had misunderstood the essentials of their own position, and that the outcome was neither victory nor defeat for either side. Take first the dispute between Galileo and the Church over the hypothesis that the sun and not the earth is the centre of the universe. There would now be almost universal agreement, first, that the Church sought to maintain an untenable doctrine of geocentrism that was quite unnecessary to its fundamental beliefs, and, second, that Galileo's theory, too, was mistaken, because we would not now recognize *any* spatial point as the absolute centre of the universe, but would measure all positions and motions relatively to some point chosen for our own convenience. Or consider the dispute over the Darwinian theory of evolution. Some Christians, again, sought to maintain an untenable and unnecessary biblical literalism, while attempts to interpret evolutionary theory in such a way as to disprove the Christian doctrine of man go far beyond anything Darwin had, or could have, shown scientifically. Indeed, the outcome of these disputes was more positive for Christian theology than absence of disproof might indicate, for they yielded greater insight into the essentials of doctrine itself, and freed it from unnecessary culture-bound complexities.

These particular disputes are no longer lively, but they have been succeeded by other controversies related to more recent science. As an example let us take Jacques Monod's attempt (in *Chance and Necessity*) to show that modern biology is incompatible with what he calls the 'anthropocentric illusion', that is, any view of the universe as permeated by purposes relevant to human life, and in which man is seen as its central product. Discussion of one such example of alleged incompatibility between Christianity and science is perhaps enough, because, as we shall see, the incompatibility is partly dependent on assumptions that are not themselves empirical discoveries, about which alternative judgements are possible and which may even be abandoned in biology itself in future paradigm changes. Such philosophical assumptions are general features of all arguments for incompatibility between science and religion, for although the content of religious belief is and ought to be influenced by the factual discoveries of science, it is never in the last resort a scientific hypothesis. And in this particular case, unlike the two cases previously mentioned, the attack is upon a non-empirical component of Christianity, which does indeed seem essential to it, namely the belief that God has purposes for man and the universe.

Monod's basic premise is what he calls the 'principle of objectivity', that is, that only scientific knowledge counts as objective knowledge. The only positive argument he gives in favour of the principle is the level of technical performance which scientific knowledge has made possible. On the basis of this argument Monod is prepared to conclude that science undermines all religious and ideological explanations that present man as being at home in the world, and specifically all ideologies (which Monod calls 'animist') that interpret the world as permeated by suprahuman purposes, including purposes for men and their history. Marxism as well as Christianity are primary examples of such animism.

Why does Monod consider that animism understood in this sense has been refuted by objective science? The answer to this question is partly technical and partly philosophical. On the technical side Monod claims that the theories of molecular biology, genetics, and evolution are now sufficiently established to make it certain that the development of living matter and its reproductive mechanisms, and the diversification of species by mutation and natural selection, are entirely governed by the operations of chance upon simpler primary material. Thus, although complex organisms like some higher mammals and man exhibit behaviour that can only be described in terms of their having purposes for their own life, this behaviour is entirely dependent on the reproductive mechanisms that ensure the survival of invariant forms of the species in successive individuals. The development of these mechanisms is wholly explicable by chance, without postulating any suprahuman purpose immanent in nature. Biology has shown, then, that purpose is parasitic upon chance, whereas all animist ideologies presuppose that purpose is primary, and even that it determines the forms of organic life. This refutation of animism, Monod thinks, explains the deep malaise of modern man, who is bereft of the value systems that seemed to be objectively supported by suprahuman purposes. Man finds himself alone in the universe, the only source of his own values and purposes, just at the time when science has given him unprecedented power to control his own environment and his history.

So much for Monod's argument. It culminates in a most moving and dignified presentation of man's dilemma, and Monod's conclusion, for which he does not claim scientific backing, is that the very practice of science itself demands moral decision, and is therefore based on an ethic of objectivity. This ethic is perhaps sufficient to replace the old ethics of animism: 'the ethic of knowledge that created the modern world is the only ethic compatible with it, the only one capable, once understood and accepted, of guiding its evolution.'[2] But can it calm the fear of solitude, satisfy the deep genetic need for an explanation in which man is at home in the universe?

I do not know. But it may not be altogether impossible. Perhaps, even more than an 'explanation' which the ethic of knowledge cannot supply, man needs to rise above himself, to find transcendence . . . No system of values can claim to constitute a true ethic unless it proposes an ideal transcending the individual self to the point even of justifying self-sacrifice, if need be.[3]

How can the 'animist', and specifically the Christian theist, reply? It would be possible of course to quibble about this or that detail of the scientific parts of Monod's argument. Some biologists will point to several as yet uncashed blank cheques in his claims for current theory; some will argue that chance plays a smaller role than he allows it, for with more information it may be that we shall see that certain of the crucial developments he discusses were determined uniquely to be as they are by the laws of matter, and are not chance developments. But whatever be the strength or conclusion of such objections, it would be unwise and even dishonest to trade on them. When a rigorous and reputable scientist claims that certain factual discoveries have been made, it is well to accept his claims in the form that gives the strongest, not the weakest, case against alternative philosophies. What it is important to discover is the *extra*-scientific assumptions that have gone into the argument, and for consideration of these, philosophical and not scientific criteria are needed. In Monod's case there are extra-scientific assumptions at every crucial point of the argument, and this means that his conclusions must be regarded as philosophical and not scientific, and judged accordingly.

The first point to notice is that any scientific theory that describes a system as developing according to probabilistic laws from some initial state is subject to two sorts of limitation on its ability to give a total explanation. First, the initial state itself is either not explained by the theory, or if it is explained by lawlike development from some other antecedent state, then *that* state is not explained, and so on. In other words, there is always some initial state that is inexplicable by a given application of any theory. In the particular case of the evolutionary history Monod describes, he entirely neglects to point out that the initial state of the primary material has to be of such a nature as to be potentially capable of producing the world as we know it, even if only as one out of many possibilities. However far we are able to go back in the history, this primary matter must have exhibited some differentiation for chance laws to operate to produce more differentiation. To see this one has only to imagine that the primary material is a wholly homogeneous continuous soup, with no qualities capable of differentiating it into parts. As Parmenides understood long ago, it is logically impossible that from such a primary unity any world of diverse qualities can come. But if no theory can explain the structure of the primary material, no theory can refute a theistic hypothesis according to which God created the world with potentialities of certain sorts of subsequent structure.

The second limitation on complete explanation applies when the laws are statistical rather than deterministic, for then successive states of the system evolve not with certainty, but only with greater or less probability from antecedent states. Any given state of the universe, together with the statistical laws believed to apply to it, is consistent with many subsequent states, each of which is assigned a certain probability by the laws. In any single system, only one of these possible outcomes is actually realized, and this may not of course even be the most probable outcome. The statistical theory itself can say nothing to explain which outcome is actualized in a single system, but can only predict of an assembly of similar systems approximately how many will yield each outcome. Now the theory of evolution seems to be a probabilistic theory, in the sense that it does not predict unique outcomes of single systems with certainty, and the overall course of evolution of life on the earth does seem to be such a single system. It is indeed a main point of Monod's argument that this evolution depends on many chance factors – chance distributions of simple molecules coming together to form organic molecules, chance mutations in favourable environments yielding new forms of life with survival value, and so on. The theory of evolution can neither explain all the chance occurrences that were necessary for this development, nor, at least in the present state of knowledge, can it predict that such a development of life and species must statistically have occurred somewhere or other in the universe. Just because chance is necessary to the evolutionary history that Monod accepts, there must be irreducibly random outcomes that scientific theory cannot explain. It follows that this theory cannot refute a theistic hypothesis according to which God is active to direct the course of evolution at points that look random from the purely scientific point of view.

So far the argument has only 'made room for' theism, and if any more positive conclusion is attempted care must be taken not to fall into a crude version of the 'God of the gaps' fallacy – postulating God where scientific explanation can go no further. The immediate objection that is likely to be raised by the agnostic is that God is here an unnecessary hypothesis for which we have no independent evidence and to which we can give no independent meaning. From the scientific point of view the hypothesis violates Occam's injunction not to multiply entities without necessity, and it is as useless as the soporific principle (*vis dormativa*) postulated by the chemists, in

Molière's quip, to explain the sleep-inducing properties of opium. Considerations quite outside science are needed before it becomes reasonable to contemplate a hypothesis that seems to be just of the kind science has rejected for three hundred years.

However, it is not only theists who require postulates based on extra-scientific considerations, and two further examples can be taken from Monod's own argument. The first of these concerns his use of the notion of 'purpose'. The only type of purpose that can be discussed by biology is that of survival of the individual and the species, and Monod claims that because this can be explained in wholly non-purposive terms by Darwinian natural selection, therefore all purpose in nature and even in human history is illusory. But this is an equivocation on 'purpose'. Human beings have many other sorts of purpose (even the lover's poem cited by Monod on page 25 *may* have a purpose other than encouragement of reproduction!). Even if it were true that biological survival does not require the purposive activity of some transcendent being or universal rational force, this would not entail that no other types of purpose are exhibited in human and animal life and its history. Indeed some biologists[4] have argued that in the higher animals and man action based on foresight may frequently have changed the environment in such a way that natural selection operates to produce ends other than simple survival. This is certainly true of man's attempts to control his future, for example by consciously reducing birth-rates in conditions of scarcity, a policy that may well result in offspring that are on the average physically weaker than those that survive the struggle for existence in an uncontrolled situation, but which better avoids the morally objectionable deaths of a high proportion of human beings in childhood. Such non-survival conditioned evolution does not seem adequately explicable by pure chance on any but the most narrowly reductionist metaphysical view.

Monod's most important philosophical presupposition is his 'principle of objectivity', namely that objective science is the only form of knowledge. He himself admits that adoption of this principle, like the adoption of any value system, is an ethical, existential decision, not itself grounded in science. It has already been noted that he does not attempt any detailed defence either of the principle, or of the brand of socialist humanism that he thinks most concordant with it. A theist might well respond by suggesting that what is sauce for the goose is sauce for the gander, and that if an ungrounded decision can responsibly be made in favour of a scientific value system and theory of knowledge, so it can for another. Specifically, it might be made for a theistic view of creation, and a value system and theory of knowledge that is consistent with this. However, such a suggestion would be valueless unless the theology, ethics and theory of knowledge can be shown to be more intimately related to each other and to what we know of the facts than Monod and other scientific humanists have been able to show in the case of their own systems.

This is a task that theology and philosophy of religion are not currently able to perform with much conviction. That it proves so difficult a task ought not to surprise us unduly, for the adoption of a unified ideology is not a matter of the intellect only, but also of pre-rational judgements of plausibility and desirability, and these are partly conditioned by surrounding culture and social institutions, particularly education. There is no need to go all the way with Marxists who reduce ideologies to mere epiphenomena of social and economic relations, in order to accept the insight of Marxism that man's reason is less free than was once believed to choose in the abstract among different intellectual systems. Scientific humanism and associated urban and industrial forms of society have had almost a monopoly in the last two hundred years in shaping human sensibilities and subjective judgements. It is not surprising that a transcendent interpretation of the world seems opaque to the intellect, even to the Christian intellect, and that it is difficult to do more than point to, and attempt to spread, what Peter Berger has called 'rumours' of the transcendent.[5] Perhaps for the foreseeable future Christian rational thought will be able to do little more in direct reply to the scientific humanist than show that even the neo-Darwinian universe leaves room for the angels. On the other hand one of the current 'rumours' is undoubtedly the widespread feeling that man is making an alien desert out of what should be, at least temporarily, his home. The attempt of this report to show how Christian insights are adequate to the understanding of this particular problem is one contribution to reasserting the relevance of the theistic hypothesis to life and action.

A SACRAMENTAL VIEW
OF NATURE[1]

by A. R. Peacocke

Although it has been common to decry from the pulpit the 'materialism' of our present age, meaning by this the current obsession with the material goods of life, it is easily overlooked that there is a sense in which the Christian faith is differentiated from other world religions by the realism of its attitude to the physical and biological character of man's existence. William Temple stressed this feature of Christian understanding in a striking passage: 'Christianity is the most materialistic of all great religions. The others hope to achieve spiritual reality by ignoring matter – calling it illusion (*maya*) or saying that it does not exist . . . Christianity, based as it is on the Incarnation, regards matter as destined to be the vehicle and instrument of spirit, and spirit as fully actual so far as it controls and directs matter.'[2] The basis of this Christian materialism he grounds firmly in the doctrine of the Incarnation: 'In the great affirmation that "the Word became flesh and we beheld his glory" (John 1:14) is implicit a whole theory of the relation between spirit and matter.'[3] From the outset Christianity was anti-Gnostic in its understanding of the material basis of men's life and its repudiation of a total other-worldliness.

However, there was a tendency amongst Christian thinkers in response to the Darwinian controversies to find their way out of the impasse then created by reverting to a naïve dualism in which the physical and biological world was assigned to science and that of 'mind' and 'spirit' to religion in general and Christianity in particular. This saved Christians from thinking too hard about the developing sciences and salved the consciences of the scientists who were thereby freed to get on with their work. This they did and the scientific and Christian communities continued, and still continue, to go their separate ways. Yet Christians should not have delegated to science all the responsibility for formulating ideas concerning the stuff, the matter, of the cosmos. For, as stressed by Temple, Christian teaching about the 'two natures' in the one 'person' of Jesus had profound implications about what was possible in the material universe which includes men's bodies and personalities. Moreover, by their character some of the central practices of the Christian faith predispose and point to, even if they do not logically compel, a certain way of regarding the material aspects of the cosmos. (This applies particularly to its sacramental use of bread, wine and water.[4])

In the Christian understanding of God's relation to physical reality, the world of matter is seen as both expressing and revealing the mind of God, its creator, and as effecting his purposes. For the physical, material world which he has brought into existence is the matrix within which and the means whereby autonomous, personal agents can be brought into existence and into harmony and union with himself. Thus, in the Christian understanding, the world of matter, in its relation to God, has both the *symbolic* function of expressing his mind and the *instrumental* function of being the means whereby he effects his purpose. We could perhaps put it thus: the created world is seen by Christians as a symbol because it is a mode of God's revelation, an expression of his truth and beauty which are the 'spiritual' aspects of its reality;[5] it is also valued by them for what God is effecting instrumentally through it, what he does for men in and through it. But these two functions of matter, the symbolical and instrumental, also constitute the special character of the use of matter in the particular Christian sacraments.[6] Hence there is, in each particular sacrament, a universal reference to this double character of created physical reality and, correspondingly, meaning can be attached to speaking of the created world as a sacrament or, at least, as sacramental. However, it must be recognized that this sacramental character is only implicit, and that it is obscure and partial both because of man's limited perception and sensitivity and because of evil. The significance of the incarnation of God in a man within the created world is that in the incarnate Christ the sacramental character of that world was made explicit and perfected. In this sense, it seems legitimate to regard the incarnate life of Christ as the supreme sacrament. For in this outward historical life, there is both uniquely expressed and uniquely operative that purpose of goodness which is the purpose of God himself that all life and all nature should fulfil.

Man in the Universe

The ability of human beings to survey their surroundings as subjects, to regard everything other than themselves as objects of their own consciousness, and so, as it were, to transcend the world, has long dominated men's view of themselves. Men have tended, and still do so, to regard their surroundings as a kind of stage on which their own personal drama is enacted, themselves in the foreground. This natural, everyday approach to the external features of man's life has played, in a variety of sophisticated forms, a dominant role in his reflections on his own nature and destiny. But in the last hundred years the perspective of the sciences concerned with the origin and development of the physical and biological worlds has altered this outlook in a way which is, or should be, changing profoundly the way man is coming to regard himself. Our familiar environments of stone, water, air, earth, grass, birds, animals, and so on, are seen both to share with us common molecular structures and to be stages in a common development in time. The very stuff of which we are made and the way it has become organized as ourselves is an inherent part of the ongoing development of the physical cosmos which we survey. We, and all other living creatures, have emerged in time out of the non-living world of water, air and rocks which seem so distinct and different from us.

Although this continuity of man with the organic world had sometimes been accepted in principle (e.g. Genesis 2:7: 'then the Lord God formed man of dust from the ground, and breathed into his nostrils the breath of life; and man became a living being'), it was not until about a hundred years ago that the scientific evidence of man's relation to other species began to appear, and it is only in the last few decades that the emergence of primitive living organisms from inorganic matter could be delineated in any fashion which had a scientific basis. This knowledge of biological evolution and of molecular biology, together with the new insights into the development of the physical cosmos which the astrophysicists and geologists are obtaining, now transpose the intimations of the writers in Genesis into the realm of well-supported scientific inference.[7]

If we are to interpret the whole cosmic development honestly, then we are bound to look at all the facts. The presence of man in the universe is just such a fact – the fact of the emergence in the cosmos of the new features and properties of matter which appear when it is organized in the form we call man. Briefly, with man evolution has become 'history', for man shapes his own physical environment and intellectual and cultural inheritance by his own choices based on his own inner drives and values which determine how he applies his unique awareness of that environment. Sir Julian Huxley calls this form of evolution 'psycho-social' although, as hinted above, the term 'history' is available for use in this sense.[8]

The new features and behaviour which have emerged in man within the cosmic development can only be described by their own appropriate language and concepts, and necessitate modes of inquiry peculiar to themselves. There are thus no grounds for rejecting, on a supposedly scientific basis, those words and modes of speaking which men have developed to describe the uniquely human experience of the world and of their understanding of themselves and their mutual relationships. Thus the language of personal relationships, of the terms used to denote intellectual and aesthetic activities, the nature of the consciousness viewed from within, all these and many more are as legitimately applied to describe and understand human beings as the language of chemistry for molecules, of physiology for the interrelation between organs in living creatures, of ethology for animal behaviour, and so on. This is not to say such language will not need to be refined and clarified, but the fact of its existence, and of the human experience which has evoked its formation, are part of the givenness of the cosmic development and cannot be ignored in any account of the cosmos which claims scientific objectivity. For the stuff of the world, the primeval concourse of hydrogen atoms or sub-nuclear particles, has as a matter of fact, and not conjecture, become man who possesses not only a social life and biological organization but also an inner life in relation to others, that which makes him personal. How are we properly to speak of the cosmic development if after aeons of time the atoms have become human beings, persons? Paradoxically, knowledge of the process by which they have arrived in the world seems to be confined to human beings. We alone reflect on our atomic and simpler forebears and we alone adjust our behaviour in the light of this perspective.

To ignore the glory, the predicament and the possibilities of man in assessing the trend and meaning of the cosmic development would be as unscientific as to endorse the former pre-Copernican account of the universe which was based on the contrary prejudice. Apparently, developing under the control of the regular processes of natural laws, new forms of matter have creatively emerged out of the nuclear particles and atoms of several thousand million years ago and have now in man become conscious both of the processes by which they have been brought into existence and of themselves. From man's consciousness new creativities of a specifically human kind have erupted, notably in men of genius but, equally significantly, in the very real individual creativity of each human being within his own social environment which, however humble, far transcends that of the highest animal. The presence of man and the fact of human personalness is therefore part of the givenness of the developing cosmos which science has unfolded.

A Sacramental View of the Cosmos

In discussing the continuity of the cosmic development, it was suggested that we need to revise what we mean by 'matter' and its associated adjective 'materialistic'. For just as the wetness of water, or the viscosity of a nucleic acid solution, are not properties of their constituent atoms but features of their higher molecular and macromolecular levels of organization, so the properties and behaviour of living organisms can be regarded as manifestations of the potentialities of matter if incorporated into certain organized structures. How such incorporation can come about and how the 'boundary conditions' of the structures are established are problems to which we have adverted already. However, once they are established, each level of organization displays its characteristic features. To be consistent, one would say that matter organized in the way we call man, notably, of course, in the labyrinth which constitutes his brain, is capable of activities which we describe as those of conscious thought, of self-reflection (self-consciousness), of communication with other human beings, and all the interrelations of personal life and ethical behaviour, of creativity in art and science and, indeed, of all the activities individual and social which characterize and differentiate man from the rest of the biological world. At each emergent level in evolution, matter in its newly evolved mode of organization manifests properties which could not, in principle, be discerned in the earlier levels from which the new emerges. In a sense, therefore, one could say that the potentialities of matter have been, and still are being, realized in the cosmic development.

However, matter has evolved into man and it seems we cannot avoid concluding, even from the most materialistic viewpoint, that the culmination of evolution in man demonstrates the ability of matter (a long-hidden potentiality now realized) to display in man functions and properties for which we have to use special terms such as 'mental', 'personal', 'spiritual'. We have to employ these special terms (which cannot, without gross qualification, be transferred even to the higher mammals) because these properties, emergent in man, are uniquely and characteristically human. Such an affirmation of, for example, the reality of human conscious and self-conscious activities, is not dependent on any particular philosophy of the relation of an entity called 'mind' to one called 'body'. This problem remains open, on this view, to philosophical analysis: it is the fact that the problem arises and can be posed on which attention is here being focused. For it seems that by taking seriously the scientific perspective we cannot avoid arriving at a view of matter which sees it as manifesting mental, personal and spiritual activities. If we were unashamedly metaphysical and were to regard these qualities as pertaining to a different mode of existence, we might reasonably describe matter as the vehicle or means of expression of this mental, personal and spiritual mode.

Whether or not we adopt this more metaphysical view of mind, persons and spirit, there is a real convergence between the implication of the scientific perspective on the capabilities of matter and the sacramental view of matter which Christians have adopted as the natural consequence of the meaning they attach to Jesus' life and the continued existence of the Church. For Christians have had to understand matter both in the light of their conviction that matter was able in the man Jesus to express the being of God, who is nevertheless regarded as supra-mental, supra-personal and supra-spiritual, so that his mode of being lies beyond any sequence of mental, etc., superlatives we can delineate; and in the light of their understanding of the sacramental acts of Jesus, made in the context of his death and resurrection, and in which the continuing life of Christian humanity originates. Briefly, it looks as if Christians, starting, as it were, from one end with their experience of God in Christ through the Holy Spirit acting in the stuff of the world, have developed an insight into matter which is consonant with that which is now evoked by the scientific perspective working from matter towards man, and beyond.

This congruence, for which I argue, between the perspective of the cosmos which science has developed and the Christian understanding of God's cosmic purposes as expressed ('symbolically') and effected ('instrumentally') through nature, the Incarnation and the eucharist is not meant to imply any identity in the way they impress themselves on us – even within the terms of Christian discourse. For science is *par excellence* a human activity in ratiocination based on experimental, empirical observations; while, for the Christian, there is a certain givenness about our encounter with God in Christ in the sacraments which cannot finally be subsumed under purely human, psychological terms.

A summary of this sacramental view,[9] which incorporates the Christian understanding of God's trinity of being and which takes seriously the scientific perspective, might be expressed thus. The world is created and sustained in being by the will of God, the will of perfect Love. The Son, the Logos, is the all-sufficient principle and form of this created order. At every level, this order reflects in its own measure something of the quality of deity. 'From atom and molecule to mammal and man each by its appropriate order and function expresses the design inherent in it and contributes, so far as it can by failure or success, to the fulfilment of the common purpose.'[10] The continuing creative power which is manifest as a nisus at all levels of existence to attain its intended form is the Holy Spirit himself.

The process of creation has been unfolded by the natural sciences as one in which new qualities and modes of existence continuously emerge out of simpler forms of matter by the operation of natural laws. The newer forms depend for their existence on the regularity of behaviour of the simpler entities out of which they are constructed but manifest properties and activities which are specific to that level of organization of matter. The level of organization which is reached in man represents not only a new summit in this evolutionary process but a new departure in the way in which change is initiated. For the mode of organization which constitutes man is characterized by activities and purposes which are only describable in terms of mind and self-consciousness. What appear to be freely willed decisions determine how the individual and society develop and how they alter their environment, which then interacts on each succeeding generation. By his intelligent apprehensions of his environment, man has become the controller and arbiter of the future of other forms of matter. He is nevertheless incomplete and unfulfilled and is tragically aware of the lack of fulfilment of his own potentialities. Thus it can be said that in man matter has become aware of itself, of its past, and of its unfulfilled potentialities.

The Christian claim, and here it differentiates itself from secular 'humanism', then amounts to the affirmation that this whole process is the outworking of the creative being of God in the world and goes on to assert further that this process has culminated in the manifestation of God as a man within the created world.[11] Only in a perfect man could God express explicitly his character as creative Love; all other levels of created being up to this point were inadequate for this purpose and but implicit manifestations of a God still *incognito*. Thus, on the one hand, that which God has brought into existence, the stuff of the cosmos, is seen through the sciences to be the matrix and necessary condition for the appearance of purpose, mind, self-consciousness and values – all that characterizes the human person; and, on the other hand, the Christian revelation affirms that this character of the stuff of the cosmos is so fundamental that God expressed his being in, and acted through, the perfect culmination of this process in the person of Jesus of Nazareth. Indeed, in Jesus we really see what personalness amounts to. The two enterprises converge in a view of the cosmos which can therefore be properly called 'sacramental'.

This technical theological term may be uncongenial to some (and not only to agnostics), but none other seems to be available which expresses so succinctly the simultaneous recognition of both the duality in our experiences represented by our familiar body-mind, subjective-objective, etc., dichotomies and the observed fact, in our own experience and in the evolutionary development revealed by the sciences, that all the 'higher' qualities of existence which characterize personal and mental life are qualities of matter in particular forms and *only* appear when matter is so organized. The term recognizes bluntly the duality necessary in our talk about ourselves and about the character of the evolutionary process, but also recognizes that the mental and spiritual features of existence are always features of, and only of, the organized matter which constitutes the observable cosmos. It is not pretended that description of the cosmos as 'sacramental' represents any real solution of the body-mind and related problems. Nevertheless, the use of this term not only avoids both idealism and the grosser forms of materialism (in the old sense) but also serves to stress the consonance between the scientific understanding of the nature of man and what Christians think is revealed of nature, man and God through the life and actions of Jesus, himself the culmination of that historical process which was at work in the Hebraic culture and which has been attested in its literature.

THE THEOLOGY OF NATURE IN THE EASTERN FATHERS AND AMONG ANGLICAN THEOLOGIANS

by A. M. Allchin

The subject of this essay is clearly too large to be treated in so small a space. The period covered by the patristic era, whether we reckon it as ending in the ninth century or later, is a very large one, the number of writers concerned is considerable, the variety of viewpoints impressive. Again, when we come to the tradition of Anglican theological writing, though the period and area is more limited, the diversity of views which has flourished among Anglican theologians is notorious. We can clearly only give a very brief and general impression of these areas, which may be of help in illustrating the background to some of the theological positions taken up in the body of the report.

1

It was a frequent comment and criticism made by Western scholars in the earlier part of this century that whereas the Western view of redemption, developing through Augustine and Anselm to the writers both Catholic and Protestant of more recent centuries, was primarily *ethical*, the view of the Eastern fathers, whether Greek or Syrian, was primarily *physical* or *natural*. In the West it has been commonly assumed that Christianity is concerned with man's personal and social existence, that it offers a way of salvation there, but that it has little or nothing to say about the existence and destiny of the universe in which man is placed. In Western terms, the effort of a Teilhard de Chardin is seen as an unusual one. It would not have seemed so unusual to the Greek fathers, even though they might have been highly critical of some of its features.

To say this is not to accept the justice of the criticism of Eastern theology, that it lacks the ethical dimension. Patristic theology, whether of East or West, centres upon man. Its concerns are existential rather than purely speculative. The whole tendency of patristic writing is to see salvation as both personal and cosmic, social and universal. This can be seen very clearly in the Easter hymns of John of Damascus, one of the greatest of later Byzantine theologians. In them the Resurrection is spoken of as being the source of life to all creation, flooding heaven and earth with light. But they also speak in a highly personal way of the believer being buried and raised with Christ, and of the Resurrection as the source of personal life and forgiveness. In this power we are to forgive even those who hate us. Ethical and natural themes are inextricably twined together, just as they are in the Old Testament psalms. Man is seen as placed at the heart of the physical world, its representative and spokesman; in the words of the title of Lars Thunberg's masterly study of Maximus the Confessor, man is seen as *Microcosm and Mediator*.

It is very striking that the same conjunction of cosmic and ethical themes is to be found in Francis' 'Canticle of the Creatures'. It would surely be wrong to see the last verse but one, even though it was added after the main body of the poem

THE THEOLOGY OF NATURE

was complete, as a kind of accidental extra. Eloi Leclerc in his study of the canticle argues strongly that, with its praise of those who make for peace, who forgive those who wrong them, who are reconciled with their neighbours, it forms a kind of completion of the earlier stanzas, with their evocation of sun and moon and stars, fire and water, earth and air. 'The will towards reconciliation which inspires and characterizes all Francis' human relations goes closely together with his attitude of brotherhood, his very deep affective communion with the most humble elements of the cosmos.' Unlike modern man, who thinks he can combine 'an attitude of respect, welcome and sympathy towards his fellow human beings, with an attitude of aggression, conquest and domination towards the whole of the rest of nature', in Francis we see a profound intuition that our attitude towards other men cannot be separated from our attitude towards other creatures. The fact that the reality of division amongst men is explicitly confronted in the canticle frees us from any temptation to see its celebration of the natural order in a sentimental or nostalgic way. 'The Franciscan vision of a brotherly universe is not a nostalgic evocation of a lost paradise. It is a vision of the world in which reconciliation prevails over division, unity over separation . . . but this unity and this fullness are not to be sought in turning back to a primitive state of sleep, but in a deeper presence to oneself and to others.'[1]

It must be said that here as in other points, although he lived after the schism of East and West, and in many respects is one of the most typically Western of saints, Francis is altogether at one with the theology and spirituality of the earlier Christian centuries. In fact his life might be seen as giving vivid expression to the theology worked out by writers such as Maximus some six centuries earlier. Commenting on this tradition, Vladimir

Lossky concludes, 'Man is not a being isolated from the rest of creation; by his very nature he is bound up with the whole of the universe, and St Paul bears witness that the whole creation awaits the future glory which will be revealed in the sons of God' (Romans 8:18-22). And Lossky goes on: 'This cosmic awareness has never been absent from Eastern spirituality, and is given expression in theology as well as in liturgical poetry, in iconography and, perhaps above all, in the ascetical writings of masters of the spiritual life of the Eastern Church. "What is a charitable heart?" – asks St Isaac the Syrian – "It is a heart which is burning with charity for the whole of creation, for men, for the birds, for the beasts, for the demons – for all creatures. He who has such a heart cannot see or call to mind a creature without his eyes being filled with tears by reason of the immense compassion which seizes his heart; a heart which is softened and can no longer bear to see or learn from others of any suffering, even the smallest pain, being inflicted upon a creature. This is why such a man never ceases to pray also for the animals, for the enemies of Truth, and for those who do him evil, that they may be preserved and purified. He will pray even for the reptiles, moved by the infinite pity which reigns in the hearts of those who are becoming united with God." In his way to union with God, man in no way leaves creatures aside, but gathers together in his love the whole cosmos disordered by sin, that it may be at last transfigured by grace.'[2]

The insistence in the passage from St Isaac, that we are to pray alike for reptiles and for our enemies, is very striking. It illustrates again the way in which man's relations with his fellow-men are seen as inseparably connected with his relations with creation as a whole; the ethical and the natural dimensions are at one. It also reveals the boldness with which the Eastern tradition has dared to think of the power of God's love to

redeem evil, even the devil. The influence of such a passage is
to be seen not only in writers such as Dostoevsky (for example,
in the Father Zossima passages in *The Brothers Karamazov*), but
also in the life and practice of contemporary Eastern monks,
amongst whom Isaac the Syrian is still one of the most respected
authorities. Examples could be multiplied of men like the
hermit Father Theoktistos on the island of Patmos, who was
renowned for the way in which he made friends with snakes.
Viewed from the Eastern Christian perspective there is nothing
eccentric or sentimental about St Francis' dealings with wolves
and fire. He is acting exactly as man does act when he is becoming integrated in himself, reconciled with the frightening
elements in his own subconscious being, advancing 'on his
way to union with God'. In such a man the creative and healing
love of God is able to be at work.

The Greek fathers of course understood man's function as
microcosm and mediator in terms of the picture of the universe
current in their own day. Things were either *noetic* or *aesthetic*,
that is to say, perceived by man's mind or spirit, or perceived
by his senses. Man was called to unite the two. He was to carry
up the material things into the realm of the spiritual, to make
the material world transparent for the spiritual. Gervase
Mathew describes this very well in relation to the Byzantine
understanding of sacred art. But what he says of man as an
artist would apply also to man as a craftsman, a technician.
'Like his friend St Gregory Nazianzen, St Gregory of Nyssa
conceived man as the bridge linking the two worlds in which
all being is divided . . . By reason of his body man belongs to
the world of matter; by reason of his soul he belongs to the
world of mind. In man alone mind and matter, the worlds of
noetos and *aisthetos*, intermingle and interpenetrate; through
man alone the material becomes articulate in the praise of God:

without him "Mind and Sense remained distinct within their
boundaries, bearing within themselves the magnificence of the
Creator Logos, but praising silently . . . Nor was there any
mingling between them; nor yet were the riches of God's
goodness manifested . . . till Man was placed on earth as a kind
of second world, a microcosm, a new angel, a mingled
worshipper . . . visible and yet intelligible, to be the husbandman of immortal plants" . . . Because man is body, he shares
in the material world around him, which passes within him
through his sense perceptions. Because man is mind he belongs
to the world of higher reality and pure spirit. Because he is
both, he is in Cyril of Alexandria's phrase "God's crowned
image"; he can mould and manipulate the material and render
it articulate.'[3]

In this vision of man as *microcosm*, placed in a central position
within the universe, it is clear that man's role is not purely
passive or contemplative. He is called to act with God in
bringing creation to its fulfilment. This active role of co-operation with the divine plan is even more underlined in the
thought of man as *mediator*, the one who gathers together the
offering of creation in order to present it to the Creator. Here
the liturgical model behind Byzantine thinking becomes particularly evident. The Liturgy itself is an offering of the world
to God by man, it is a passing over; in no sense a static thing,
but rather a movement from this world into the world to come,
from earth to heaven. In the thought of Maximus the Confessor,
for example, the whole of mankind and indeed the whole
universe is conceived to be in some way associated with this
movement of offering, this coming to God. The Greek fathers,
in common with the whole world of thought in which they
lived, do not think of this movement in historical terms, but as
Fr Staniloae suggests in his commentary on the *Mystagogia* of

Maximus, there is no reason why we should not develop their thought in this direction, and see the whole process of evolution, the whole process of human history, as a gradual movement, a slow, and at times painful, ascent towards the Kingdom.

2

'All Christian life is sacramental. Not alone in our highest act of Communion are we partaking of heavenly powers through earthly signs and vehicles. This neglected faith may be revived through increased sympathy with the earth derived from fuller knowledge, through the fearless love of all things.'[4]

The words are those of an outstanding nineteenth-century theologian, who was also a practising natural scientist. The 'neglected faith' of which they speak is one which has been present, more or less evidently, in a large part of Anglican thinking, at least since the end of the sixteenth century. This particular way of seeing all things as potentially sacramental, and of maintaining that that which is distinctively Christian can only be understood in relation to things which are not specifically so, might be said to be one of the distinguishing marks of Anglican theology, as compared with the thought of the Continental Reformation. To quote Hort again, 'Christianity consists of the most central and significant truth concerning the universe, intelligible only in connection with other truth not obviously Christian, and accepted by many not Christian.'[5] Whereas the basic method of most Reformation thinking is to proceed by way of an either/or, grace or nature, God or man, the Church or the Bible, the Anglican tradition has tried always to proceed by way of both/and, holding together things apparently opposed.

149

This fact is not simply the result of the accidents of history. It stems from the nature of the thought of the most profound and most influential of Anglican theologians at the time of the Reformation, Richard Hooker; for Hooker thinks in terms of conjunction rather than disjunction, of mutual participation rather than mutual exclusion. He sees the one wisdom of God shining 'in the beautiful variety of all things', not only 'in the manifold and yet harmonious dissimilitude' of the ways in which God has guided his Church at different times, but also in the infinitely varied expressions of God's creative power with which the universe is filled.[6]

When we turn to Hooker's teaching about creation itself, we can see that he must have been well aware of the dangers of a purely external view of God's relation to the world which are mentioned in Chapter 2 of this report. Without holding an emanationist view of creation he seems concerned to safeguard all that is valuable within it. 'God hath his influence into the very essence of all things, without which influence of Deity supporting them their utter annihilation could not choose but follow. Of him all things have both received their first being and their continuance to be that which they are. All things are therefore partakers of God, they are his offspring, his influence is in them, and the personal wisdom of God is for that very cause said to excel in nimbleness or agility, to pierce into all intellectual, pure, and subtile spirits, to go through all, and to reach unto every thing which is.'[7] 'So that all things which God hath made are in that respect the offspring of God, they are in him as effects in their highest cause, he likewise is actually in them, the assistance and influence of his Deity is their life.'

We have here a teaching which stresses that God has not only made things in the beginning, but that he constantly continues to hold them in being; that he is not only their maker and fashioner from outside, but that his power and influence maintain them from within. Such teaching is influenced by the scholastic tradition and is derived in part from St Thomas Aquinas' statement that God is 'in all things by essence, presence and power'.[8] This teaching in Hooker about the relationship of the world to God is set in Hooker's argument between his discussion of the mutual participation of the persons of the Holy Trinity amongst themselves, and his discussion of the mutual participation of Christ and the Church. This means that his interest is not merely or even primarily cosmological, but it also means that his doctrine of redemption is inseparably connected with his doctrine of creation. The understanding of the incarnation and the sacraments of Christ is linked to the understanding of God's creative action in all things.

Hence in his controversy with the Puritans, Hooker can maintain that God does not speak to us only through scripture, but in a great variety of ways, through reason, law, the tradition of the Church and the experience of the nations. Not only in our specifically religious actions do we please God, nor shall we truly please him in them, unless we know that at all times and in many modes his glory is revealed. 'We move, we sleep, we take the cup at the hand of our friend, a number of things we oftentimes do, only to satisfy some natural desire, without present, express, and actual reference unto any commandment of God. Unto his glory even these things are done which we naturally perform, and not only that which morally and spiritually we do. For by every effect proceeding from the most concealed instincts of nature his power is made manifest.'[9] Prayer itself is not to be confined to acts of prayer explicitly made. 'Every good and holy desire, though it lack the form, hath notwithstanding in itself the substance and with him the force of a prayer, who regardeth the very moanings, groans, and sighs of the heart of man.'[10] 'Not alone in our highest act of Communion are we partaking of heavenly powers through earthly signs and vehicles.'

This was the theology which lay behind the teaching of many Anglicans during the seventeenth century, and at least during its first fifty years it was supported by a view of the world in which man was still seen as a microcosm, a little world containing all the elements in miniature. This sense of the interpenetration of man and nature declined quickly in the latter part of the century, under the impact of the new scientific thinking. By the time when he wrote in the 1670s, the ecstatic prose of Thomas Traherne had already begun to sound strange and anachronistic. But the 'theology of conjunction', which stemmed from Hooker's work, was not bound to any one world-view. Its influence had been felt in the seventeenth century among Cambridge Platonists as well as Laudians, and it continued to be felt in the latter part of the century among some of the leaders of the scientific movement themselves, most notably Robert Boyle and John Ray. Its basis was a 'via media which was not in its essence compromise or an intellectual expedient but a quality of thinking, an approach in which elements usually regarded as mutually exclusive were seen to be in fact complementary. These things were held in a living tension, not in order to walk the tight-rope of compromise, but because they were seen to be mutually illuminating and to fertilize each other.'[11] Things which were 'held together' in this way included the Church's traditional faith, and the free exercise of rational inquiry; teaching about the specific sacraments of the faith, and belief in the sacramental potentiality of all things.

So it was that in the eighteenth century this approach did not wholly disappear in the Anglican tradition. It came to life again at the end of the century in poetic form in the writings of Wordsworth and of Coleridge, whose sacramental vision of the natural world provided the context in which the rediscovery of the specifically sacramental nature of Christian worship took place. In Coleridge, indeed, it found a thinker who was in the nineteenth century the unacknowledged inspiration of schools of thought as diverse as those of Keble and Newman on the one side, and Westcott and Hort on the other. Particularly in the case of the latter we can see the conjunction of traditional faith with a critical approach to Christian origins, the desire to bring together an understanding of Christ's redemptive action with the new insights into the nature of the physical universe which were being opened up by the natural sciences.

In *Lux Mundi* these two schools of thought converged, and in that collection of essays there are more than a few signs which point towards the emergence of a new theology of the sanctification of matter. 'And so', writes Francis Paget, 'through sacramental elements and acts Christianity maintains its strong inclusive hold upon the whole of life . . . We seem to see the material world rising from height to height; pierced, indeed, and, as it were, surprised at every stage by strange hints of a destiny beyond all likelihood; yet only gradually laying aside the inertness of its lower forms, gradually seeming to yield itself, not merely to the external fashioning of spirit, but also to its inner and transforming occupation: till in humanity it comes within sight of that which God has been preparing for it, even the reception of his own image and likeness.'[12]

Still more striking is Charles Gore's exposition of Christology in his Bampton lectures of 1891, *The Incarnation of the Son of God*. While in no way minimizing the transcendent element in the Incarnation, he roots the event of Christ firmly in the development of the natural order and the course of human history. The former Archbishop of Canterbury, Dr Michael Ramsey, in his book *From Gore to Temple*, summarizes his argument thus: 'Nature represents an order and a unity, and also a progress . . . In inorganic nature is seen his [God's] immutability, power and wisdom: in organic nature he has shown that he is alive; in human nature he has given glimpses of his mind and character. "In Christ not one of those earlier revelations is abrogated, nay they are reaffirmed. But they reach a completion in the fuller exploration of the divine character, the divine personality, the divine love." '13

Again in the twentieth century this tradition has reasserted itself in writers as different as Charles Raven on the one side, or L. S. Thornton on the other. It inspired much of the writing of one of the outstanding churchmen of our century, William Temple. It has undoubtedly influenced the general approach to theological questions which is reflected in this report, and has found notable new expression in the writings of one of the members of this group.

This brief excursus into Anglican history is not meant to suggest that the unprecedented questions which confront us at the end of the twentieth century are to be resolved by an appeal to precedents from the past. It is to suggest that, did we but know our tradition better, we might discover in it some unexpected resources for working out a theology of the environment. The characteristics which have been dominant in Western Christian thought, and which the ecological crisis has brought us to question, are sometimes precisely those characteristics where, from within the theological tradition, Anglican thinkers have been inclined to dissent from their often more numerous and powerful contemporaries.

ON 'THE HISTORICAL ROOTS OF OUR ECOLOGICAL CRISIS'

by A. R. Peacocke

The above is the title of a much-quoted essay[1] in which Lynn White urges that the exploitative outlook which has engendered the ecological crisis in Western industrialized nations is itself the direct result of the Judeo-Christian tradition which, he says, basing itself on Genesis 1:28, has conceived of man as superior to and dominant over nature which, in this tradition, he claims, 'has no reason for existence save to serve man'. Indeed, he calls this last a 'Christian axiom'. The article has been widely quoted and its argument accepted by those who are only too eager to find yet another stick with which to beat Christianity (even if, ironically, only yesterday they were deploring Christianity's supposed dogmatic antagonism to science and technology!), and by those Christians, such as Lynn White himself, who accept it more in sorrow than in anger in hope that the Church might then emerge purified from its sackcloth and ashes to provide the moral lead for ecological renewal.[2]

That there have been and are Western Christians who hold this particular constellation of beliefs and that at some times and places they may even have been held by a majority of Christians seems quite likely. But to substantiate White's hypothesis, which has been made even more dogmatic and has been more widely generalized by others, it would be necessary to show that men in the 'Judeo-Christian tradition' have uniquely generated the eco-disasters of our planet; that an exploitative view of nature was actually and generally held in that tradition; and that this tradition actually does involve such an exploitative view. In fact, none of these three statements can be adequately substantiated and the hypothesis also emerges as much too simplistic. We shall indicate very briefly why this is so.

Firstly, it is quite clear that man's exploitation of his natural environment, leading to irreversible ecological changes of a kind inimical to the welfare of subsequent generations of men, has occurred from the time of primitive man onwards and is not specifically associated with Judeo-Christian societies. Long before the Jewish prophets and the advent of Jesus primitive man had hunted by 'fire-drive' methods and Mediterranean man had stripped the trees and turned into barren terrain both the hills and plains of much of the lands bordering that sea. Disastrous interference with nature is not confined to the Christian West as a visit to modern industrial Japan quickly establishes.

Secondly, even among the followers of the Judeo-Christian[3] tradition there have been marked divergences between their attitudes to science and technology – which, broadly speaking, developed most in the Latin form of Christianity of Western Europe and, more particularly, found their most congenial climate in the Protestant variant of that form. Technology never flourished in the Orthodox Byzantine Empire of the East, although – just to controvert all attempts at historical generalizations – it did develop strongly in the non-Christian cultures of China, and both science and technology have distinct roots in ancient Greece and medieval Islam.

Even with reference to Western Latin Christianity, it cannot be maintained that the exploitative, rapacious attitude to nature was uniformly encouraged in a society which could produce both a St Francis, with his sense of oneness with all the creatures and creations of God, and a St Benedict who, through the working symbiotic communities that he initiated, fostered the habit of an ordered balanced interplay with natural cycles which increased the fertility and fecundity of the areas where Benedictines and Cistercians settled.

The Western medieval bestiaries testify not only to the interest of a more rural society in all kinds of living creatures, but also to the *meaning* which was attributed to everything in a universe that was governed by a controlling mind and was capable of rational explanation. For example, the activities of some animals are seen as types of Christ and of others as moral lessons for man. Moreover: 'The Bestiary is a compassionate book. It has its bugaboos, of course, but these are only there to thrill us. It loves dogs, which never was usual in the East from which it originated; it is polite to bees, and even praises them for being communists like the modern Scythians [the Russians of their day]; it is tender to poor, blind Echinus [the sea-urchin]; the horse moves it, as Sidney's heart was moved, "more than with a trumpet"; above all, it has a reverence for the wonders of life, and praises the Creator of them: in whom, in those days, it was still possible absolutely to believe.'[4]

Thirdly, the Judeo-Christian tradition, at least as represented in its main written documents, the Bible, does not, in fact, depict man's dominion over nature as simply brutally exploitative, as if nature is there only for man's benefit. As with all the neat headings within which theological discourse would like to confine the richly variegated books of the Bible, it is almost impossible to produce a 'biblical doctrine' of nature and man's relation to it. The evidence has been widely surveyed[5] in relation to ecological concerns, not to mention the more standard works on the theology of the Bible[6] – and these have been important considerations elsewhere in this report. But briefly, it is clear that the dominion afforded to man in Genesis 1:28 is a dominion exercised under God and that man who exercises this dominion is responsible to God, for 'the earth is the Lord's' and not man's. Man is a trustee, steward and manager for that which is not his own and which is of value for its own sake to God, for God delights in *all* that he has made and not in man alone. It is true that, in the Old Testament, nature is de-sacralized and is not to be worshipped, but it has value, that which God gives it by calling it into being.

For these broad reasons, the evidence scarcely seems to justify Lynn White in asserting that 'Christianity bears a huge burden of guilt' (for the possession by man of technological powers now out of control) or in speaking of the 'orthodox Christian arrogance toward nature'. In spite of cogent criticisms[7] of Lynn White's hypothesis, it has been favourably quoted by many environmentally concerned authors. Even though, in the light of the evidence, one cannot agree with his analysis of the roots of our present situation, at least it is clear that one must eschew this particular complex of ideas which Christians, no doubt, are more prone to use to rationalize their cupidity than would be non-Christians (who probably have other psychological devices at their call).

SOME EVIDENCE
FROM OTHER RELIGIONS

Compiled by Don Cupitt

From the outset the group recognized that it would be necessary to review material from non-Christian religions about the relation of man to nature. But it soon became clear that an adequate comparative study of man and nature in the religions would be an immense task, which no single scholar has yet attempted. Instead we offer here a few extracts from memoranda written for us, in which points of special interest are made.

It is sometimes supposed that only modern, industrial man devastates his environment. This is not true. There are large areas of the world which were made into deserts by overgrazing, by bad agricultural practices, and so on, in ancient times. Professor Monica Wilson reminded us, in correspondence, that it is a mistake to imagine that even small-scale tribal societies invariably lived in ideal ecological harmony with their environment; even though the religions of such societies are very closely tied to the rhythms of nature. She writes as follows: 'I can make two comments for small societies in Africa which probably hold more widely.

'(a) Generally in Africa there is a lively awareness of the dead, and of the obligations of the living to them. I believe that a sense of obligation to those to come is connected with this.

'(b) There is an obligation not to squander wealth inherited from the shades but rather to use it and transmit it. This is very clear among cattle people regarding "lineage cattle", which are rarely killed for food, but regularly as offerings to the shades. To hold feasts for the shades – a communion of kin – was a moral duty. But hunting people who acquired stock had no comparable inhibitions about slaughtering it; they ate their breeding stock when they were hungry. There are indications, however, that at least some hunters conserved their resources of roots and nuts, and perhaps even of game.

'Among cultivators limitations on destroying or disposing of land sometimes existed. In Ghana lineage land was distinguished from personally acquired land, and the rights of disposal over the two sorts differed.

'I do not think that these ideas differed radically from ideas in England about responsibility for entailed estates, or ideas (obvious in my parents' generation and still alive in mine) about not "spending capital" but transmitting wealth inherited to the next generation.

'René Dumont of Paris, in a recent lecture at the university here, contrasted a Kirdi's reply (in the Cameroons) with that of an American in Hawaii. The Kirdi, when asked to whom the land belonged, said "It belongs to our ancestors, whom we respect; to the people living now, who may clear fields to grow their food; and to their progeny until the end of the world, and for whom we must keep the soil in good condition." The American admitted that when sugar-cane was grown on very steep slopes and harvested with bulldozers, erosion could sweep away the soil within thirty years. "But", he said, "in thirty years we have made a profit ten times more than the price we paid for the field." Dumont implied (though he did not say it) that preliterate man was more likely to be responsible about land than modern industrial man. I don't think this is true.

'Cattle peoples in Africa in the past fifty years have destroyed much of their pasture-land by over-grazing. They think in terms of looking after their breeding stock, and doing the best they can for it immediately, not in terms of the land. I believe that in past time deserts have spread in Africa for this reason. There is some evidence that the Masai steppe was once fertile; the Karroo is spreading eastward owing to "bad farming" by both white and black; the Kalahari was spreading *before* whites came. In short, the notion that "the savage" is always noble is a myth.

'Ancient civilized peoples also destroyed their land: was not much of north Africa which is now desert once the granary of Rome? And the flooding of the Yangtze from which China has suffered for so long was due to the felling of forests on steep slopes in Yunnan. The Maya in South America are also said to have destroyed land by their methods of cultivation.

'From this I conclude that particular groups at particular times have shown a lively sense of responsibility for inherited resources; others have not. And a rise in population may mean that techniques which once did little damage become destructive. This was true of slash-and-burn cultivation (swidden) in parts of Zambia in the 1940s.

'I think that the difficulty lies in adapting moral obligations to a changing environment. In the Keiskammahoek district of South Africa, in the 1950s, agriculturalists and economists were trying desperately to get villagers to sell or eat their cattle, which were too many for the grazing, but at the initiation rituals for young men the admonition was still: "Don't squander your earnings on riotous living; build up the homestead; buy cattle!" Many good sons did so, losing the stock in the next drought.'

Small-scale societies, then, can be ecologically improvident, and their religion can be an obstacle; but it is fair to add that our activities nowadays are more dangerous because they are on a larger scale, and more culpable in that we are more aware than our ancestors of the likely dangers of, for example, destroying the remaining tropical rain-forests.

Dr Kenneth Cragg contributed a valuable note about Islam, a faith in which the idea of man as God's viceroy or steward appears in a form interestingly like and unlike the more familiar Judeo-Christian doctrine. He writes:

'Though the theme may not be articulate in popular Islam the theme of man as "steward" in nature is certainly basic to the Quranic doctrine of the human condition. It turns, essentially, on two related concepts: (1) the *khalīfah* role of man; and (2) the sense of the "signs" or *āyāt*.

'The pivotal passage is one of the several that deal with the creation of man. God announces that he is setting or appointing a *khalīfah* in the earth (Surah 2.30). The word means "one who takes the place of" another, either as a "successor" or a "deputy". God having no "successors", the sense of one in charge on behalf of God must be meant. True, there has been some reluctance in Muslim exegesis to accept that man could "deputize" for God even in this limited sense. Such exegetes have, therefore, seen Adam as merely one with successors, the "caliphate" of man being merely the temporal succession of human generations from Adam. But this limited purely human meaning cannot fit the whole passage in 2.30. It is clear that much more than mortal sequences are meant. For the angels demur at the idea of entrusting the creation to so fickle and frail a creature, who can be relied on only to thwart and distort the divine design in the world. Why not an angelic hegemony over things? But God sticks to his purpose and requires the angels to "worship" Adam (the verb normally used only for worship of God), meaning that the angels are to acknowledge the human dignity as divinely willed. Satan, or the devil, continues in a solitary defiance of God and refuses to prostrate himself to the creature. So he is banished and it becomes his aim in history to tempt the human creature, so as to discredit the divine scheme and prove to God the folly of ennobling man. (This is very much in line with "the accuser" of Job 1-2 – the discreditor of mankind.)

'In this eloquent form of myth, man is seen as entrusted with the care of the earth, on behalf of God. He is God's vice-regent or vicegerent, exercising "dominion" *over* the material order, that he may thus be the "servant" (*'abd*) of the divine law. Man is thus servant-master and is not rightly thought of as either, except in being both. The raw material of his technology is the arena of his adoration of God. He consecrates what he rules and only does either in doing both.

'Elsewhere in the Quran this idea of entrustment of the universe (the term is the *amānah*) is the deep contrast between the human sphere, and the inanimate and animal creation. Man is both responsible and accountable. This is the context of his *islām* or due acknowledgement of God. Sometimes the orderliness of the planets and of chemical reactions, etc., is seen as a kind of cosmic physical *islām* – an involuntary sub-ordination; but man's vocation to the recognition of law is volitional and requires an active, rational, purposive, chosen *islām*, or conformity. To educate and ensure this is the religious business of Islam proper.

'I have no doubt that this dominion theme is the Quranic clue in the contemporary concern for the environment.

'The other salient idea is that of the *āyāt*, or signs. Nature is a sphere of hints, intimations, disclosures, of divine mercy. In experiencing the physical order – harvest, pregnancy, wells, winds, flowers, and so on – one is really at the point of convergence of a physical realm and a spiritual. There are purely empirical causation links but these are the points of awareness of God's goodness and provision. Whereas the casual see only the external phenomena, the reverent see the goodness and the significance. So all experience is "arresting", i.e. summoning us to discernment and attentiveness. Science proceeds by curiosity responding to ascertainable significance. True religion proceeds by apprehending the meaning. Such apperception evokes gratitude. When the "signs" are greeted, worship is released. Thus, in a way, all our awareness is awareness of the "sacramental". The Quran is constantly calling men to thankfulness – a gratitude responsive to a *felt* significance.'[1]

The oriental religions pose the severest problems of all. A great deal of valuable evidence is scattered through the volumes of Dr Joseph Needham's monumental work *Science and Civilization in China*.[2] Professor Ninian Smart offered us brief guidelines, suggesting that in Indian thought the distinctions between the living and the non-living, and between man and animals, are less clear-cut than we are accustomed to. He writes:

'First, we may note that a less clear distinction is made in the Indian tradition between physical nature and living beings than has been customary in recent Western thought. This is brought out by the fact that most frequently mental functions and feelings and so forth are regarded as being material, i.e. made of subtle forms of the matter which constitutes the basis of the whole of nature. A sharp distinction on the other hand tends to be drawn between the soul as an eternal entity and the psycho-physical organism plus physical nature. This sharp distinction is in part the background of the other-worldliness of Indian asceticism. It may also be noted that the physical universe contains not merely mundane living beings but gods as well, and in some aspects of Hindu thinking and in Buddhist thought even the great God Brahmā is considered an inhabitant of the cosmos. In this respect the Creator himself needs to be transcended. All this being so, there is a less developed sense of nature as over against God and the gods. Incidentally, it is in my view wrong to speak of pantheism in this connection and I know of no Indian system which is strictly speaking pantheistic.

'A further point of interest in relating man to the natural environment is that the division between man and other animals is less sharp than in the West. Indeed, there is a whole range of living beings of whom man is but one sort. There are gods of various kinds, spirits, ghosts, men, monkeys, birds, and so forth. The shock provided by evolutionary theory to Western consciousness arose partly from the strict division between man and animals and no doubt also from the association of sexuality and violence with animals (our language includes terms like "brute", "bestial practice", "animal behaviour", "beastly", etc.). On the other hand evolutionary theory did not have any strong socio-psychological impact on the Indian scene. We may note also that the valuation of animals is sometimes higher than the valuation of some men or even all men. Thus cows and monkeys are sacred and highly reverenced. The continuum between man and other forms of life is reinforced by the doctrine of rebirth. Thus one can be reincarnated as a god or as a worm, and so forth.

'Connected is the value known as *ahimsā*, or non-injury. This is stressed very rigorously in Jainism, and strongly in

Buddhism and at varying times in the Hindu tradition – notably in recent times by Gandhi. The effect of this attitude towards animals and men varies from culture to culture but undoubtedly has some effect in restraining people, in, for example, Ceylon, from wantonly slaughtering animals. There is also of course a strong vegetarian strain in the Indian tradition.

'Although these values are strongly embedded in Indian religious consciousness it would be unwise to assume that these values necessarily have very powerful practical consequences (though cow-preservation remains pervasive in India). On the aesthetic side probably the strongest sense of communion with animals and nature is to be found in certain early Buddhist writings.

'Some of these attitudes were taken by Buddhism into China, where they spread and coalesced in some degree with attitudes discoverable in the Taoist tradition. The very notion that there is a principle pervading the universe with which one can be in harmony gives a distinctive flavour to much of Chinese thought and art. In the case of Taoism there was stress on the way in which nature acts by not acting and so man too should act by non-action. This passive and sometimes politically anarchistic teaching coincides somewhat with Buddhist emphases upon contemplation and non-violence. A synthesis was achieved in Ch'an Buddhism, later to be transmuted into Japanese in the form of Zen. Perhaps the Chinese stressed less than the Indian tradition the hierarchy of living beings in the universe but it certainly more prominently expressed the feeling of communion with nature, and with principles governing the weather, landscape, and so forth. Both in India and in China the rituals of geomancy indicate a certain caution as well as a certain gentleness in the way in which one must treat the natural order when one is completing a house or otherwise disturbing the ground. Partly because preceding Japanese culture prepared the way, for Shinto divinities were already closely associated with natural features and places and forces, the aesthetic attitudes of Taoism and Buddhism had a marked effect upon Japanese culture.

'Though the idea of creation is certainly quite prominent in certain phases of Eastern cultures, nevertheless it has a different placing than in the West and thus one major conclusion of this short account is that there is less in the way of sharp separations in the hierarchy of being, and this is one major reason for a different attitude to nature. In addition, the strongly contemplative strand both in Indian religions and in Taoism helps to account for the attitude of non-injury.'

Finally, Professor John Bowker reminded us of how complex the relation of religion to culture is; and of how many-sided, within each major tradition, the doctrines and attitudes may be. Not only in the case of Christianity, but in other cases too, we may find elements of concern for the world, of indifference to its fate, and of rejection, all strangely tangled. If the group has sought to search and reinterpret the Christian tradition, similar operations can be, perhaps should be, carried out in other traditions. But inter-faith consensus will not easily be reached:

'It is obvious that all religions can make some response to the issues and problems of ecology, and since religions remain the contexts, or universes of meaning, in which the majority of human beings live their lives, and from which they derive resources for the construction of those lives, it is perhaps important that religions should be encouraged to make that response. Furthermore, it is possible that if the problems of survival become even more acute, their spokesmen will be found speaking with a large (though probably very general) measure of uniformity. But this must not be allowed to obscure the fact that the differences between those different universes of meaning are, or can be, profoundly competitive and divisive.'

MARXISM, NATURE AND WORK

by Paul Oestreicher

Marxism a century after Marx is as diverse and divided as Christianity. This attempt, by a sympathetic but critical Christian student of Marxism, to describe the Marxist contribution to the debate about man in his environment cannot possibly hope to satisfy all Marxists. There is a genuine debate within Marxism, a debate still in its infancy, which this short paper can only marginally reflect. It does not claim to be totally objective. It does try to be fair. Some insight into the current debate may be gained by studying contributions in *Marxism Today*, March–May and July 1974.

If the great growth debate, arising from an overwhelming and sudden recognition that a fundamental disharmony exists between the planet earth and the human beings who 'rule' it, has caught Christians unawares and has only just begun to concern the Churches seriously, the same can – broadly speaking – be said of communists and communist parties. The reasons are almost exactly the same and are to be found, in both cases, in a common heritage. The Hebrew-Christian tradition from which communism sprang (and against parts of which it reacted) firmly enthrones man as a plenipotentiary being within the created order. The concept that it is man's God-given duty and privilege to subdue the earth and make it fruitful is fundamental to a Christian understanding of man in relation to nature. The philosophy of the Enlightenment to which Marx was also heir thought it immature to remain wedded to an unverifiable creator, exterior to the discernible universe. But it did not follow that the natural order was a haphazard, anarchic accident. It was assumed that the laws of its existence were immanent in creation and could be discovered by man, who in discovering scientific reality was also setting himself free. Freedom for man was the recognition of (scientific) necessity.

Not altogether surprisingly the parallel development of a theology centred on God incarnate in human history and the communist theory of man's autonomy in the process of establishing his mastery over the scientific order meant that in both nominally Christian and nominally communist developed countries there were no ideological reasons for curbing scientific and technological 'progress'.

J. D. Bernal, the communist scientist and historian of science, summed up this whole philosophic position from a traditional Marxist point of view: '. . . we have in the practice of science the prototype for all human common action. The task which the scientists have undertaken – the understanding and control of nature and of man himself – is merely the conscious expression of the task of human society. The methods by which this task is attempted, however imperfectly they are realized, are the methods by which humanity is most likely to secure its own future . . . In science men have learned consciously to subordinate themselves to a common purpose without losing the individuality of their achievements. Each one knows that his work depends on that of his predecessors and colleagues, and that it can only reach its fruition through the work of his successors. In science men collaborate not because they are forced to by superior authority or because they blindly follow some chosen leader, but because they realize that only in this willing collaboration can each man find his goal. Not orders,

but advice, determines action . . . because such advice expresses
as near as may be the inexorable logic of the material world,
stubborn fact. Facts cannot be forced to our desires, and freedom comes by admitting this necessity . . . These are things
that have been learned painfully and incompletely in the pursuit of science. Only in the wider tasks of humanity will their
full use be found.'[1]

In this same context J. D. Bernal is prepared actually to say
that, in its endeavour, 'science is communism'. And communism, it must be remembered, is – in Marxist understanding
if not terminology – an eschatological concept as well as a
political system. In other words man's mastery of science is
potentially his liberation, his perfectly fulfilled life both
personally and corporately. Marxism has however never fully
faced the complex implications of the fact that man is both
part of natural scientific reality and its discoverer. Perhaps the
most controversial contribution of nineteenth-century Marxism
to contemporary thought has been the conviction (drawn by
Engels from some of Marx's writings) that man in society
could be studied just as scientifically as atoms in relation to
molecules. But is there such a thing as social and political
science? Can man objectively know himself individually and
corporately? Communism, assuming this to be possible, sees
itself as scientific and therefore true or, in its own terminology,
'correct'. But it should by now be self-evident that the moment
a canon of scientific (or revealed) truth is declared man will, by
nature, discover rival truths and so create schism. There is no
orthodoxy without its concomitant heresies. In consequence
there is today no single communist view on any important
problem, any more than there is a single Christian view; not,
that is, if one proceeds beyond commonly held general pro-
positions to their specific application.

If there is an integral sociological link between Western religion and the rise of capitalism – and I accept that there is – then one might imagine that the communist reaction against capitalism and religion might have been even more radical than it has proved to be. Communism in theory and practice has not condemned the creation of capital by the industrial process and the harnessing of millions of men to it, but has merely affirmed that if the means of production and distribution are put into the hands of the people, then labour will no longer need to be an alienating process but will in time become a liberating fulfilment of man's creative potential.

For Hegel, labour was man's act of self-creation. Marx accepted that, and his political philosophy is almost solely concerned with demonstrating that this can become true in experience. The nature of animals is eternal repetition, that of man is transformation, development, change. An animal is the past incarnate in the present; man is not only past and present but also future. An animal accepts what nature offers; man forces nature to give him more. He lays hands on nature, enters into conflict with it, alienates himself from it and takes possession of what has become alien by making it serve its purpose, by *working* it. Man works himself out of nature, forming his own personality by his hands, his consciousness and his imagination in community with other men. What then is labour? 'Labour is, in the first place, a process in which both man and nature participate, and in which man of his own accord starts, regulates, and controls the material reactions between himself and nature . . . By thus acting on the external world and changing it, he at the same time changes his own nature . . . We presuppose labour in a form that stamps it as exclusively human . . . What distinguishes the worst architect from the best of bees is this, that the architect raises his structure in imagination before he erects it in reality.'[2]

All this presupposes, in Marx, total respect for the integrity of nature's laws. Lack of such respect would be unscientific. Comparably, Christians might be expected to have a similar respect for the natural order because they hold God's creation in awe. In practice, however, the doctrine of the primacy of man (whether absolutely or only 'under God') left Marxist communists and Christian capitalists virtually without restraint in their assault on nature. In consequence reality has caught up with society and capitalist and communist systems alike are beginning to reel under the shock of nature beginning to 'get its own back'. Man cannot limitlessly force nature to give him more. And so it is now no longer surprising that the United Nations can get governments to agree to a world conference on the protection of the environment and of the human species within it. The earth simply will not be limitlessly raped. Marx, to his considerable credit, did predict this, although in strictly ideological terms. 'Capitalist production . . . disturbs the circulation of matter between man and the soil . . . all progress in capitalist agriculture is a progress in the art, not only of robbing the labourer, but of robbing the soil; all progress in increasing the fertility of the soil for a given time, is a progress towards ruining the lasting sources of that fertility. The more a country starts its development on the foundation of modern industry, like the United States, for example, the more rapid is this process of destruction. Capitalist production, therefore, develops technology, and the combining together of various processes into a social whole, only by sapping the original sources of all wealth – the soil and the labourer.'[3]

These strictures apply equally, of course, to developments since 1918 in the Soviet Union. Only now are Soviet scientists

– with Western ones – prepared to concede that industry need not be an unmixed blessing and that the exploitation of natural resources must be governed by laws yet to be determined. Self-critical Marxist voices are now being heard, not openly decrying communist praxis but recognizing that true communism requires radical and undogmatic rethinking. In this context the concept of a third industrial revolution, one which would consciously change the whole basis of production to ecologically sound methods, not simply change the social and economic relations to suit a system of production that was already there, will need to be at the centre of the building of a communist society. 'The socialist revolution is unlike any other in history; it is the first to be *consciously made* and unlike others will involve the conscious transformation of the whole of society, of man's relationship to man *and to the environment*, a revolution not only in the social relations of production, but in the techniques and nature of production as well. The immediacy of current problems requires that this receives more attention than the constraints which sometimes operate on our own thinking have sometimes allowed us to give it.'[4] /

Communism in Russia and Eastern Europe from 1917 until now cannot yet be said to have faced these issues seriously – any more than can capitalism in America and Western Europe. What can properly be said is that *theoretically* Marxism is a little better placed to make the necessary sacrifices. It allows for them, and in fact demands them in the interests of an ultimate harmony between man and his environment in which there will be a perfect balance between need and its fulfilment. At present the contradictions between the claim to know scientifically what is good for man and actual social conditions in Eastern Europe are so glaring that many in the West are convinced that communism is wholly irrelevant. If the present crisis of capitalism develops further, I suspect that this facile view of communism will be much more difficult to maintain.

But more importantly, what little we know of the social, agricultural and industrial development of China over the last generation suggests that Maoism, at any rate, may not show the glaring contradictions of Western communism and capitalism. China has resolutely refused to industrialize at the expense of the land, or to employ vast technological schemes when intermediate technology provides better solutions. China claims that a vast population is creatively employed and materially given a basic security never before known. And all this without foreign aid. Significantly there is, in Maoist writing, very little theoretical work about man, labour and nature. There are simply the basic Chinese philosophic assumptions, and the Marxist assumptions, that there must be a fundamental harmony between them. Closest attention must be given to the social and scientific realities. In other words there can be no doctrinal prescription but only the application of experience to new attempts to increase creative living. Importantly this is not, in China, held to imply a need for greatly increased consumption, or even production. Right social relationships and a proper evaluation of natural needs (rather than needs stimulated by enforced productivity of commodities) are held to take precedence. It is therefore not altogether surprising that the Chinese think that the Western debate about growth, technology and pollution hardly touches their basic problems at all.

It may legitimately be doubted whether the communists in power in Eastern Europe have sufficient credibility to recapture and reinterpret Marxist insights in ways which will be creatively relevant to the whole of the 'developed' world. Infinitely more important, however, is the Marxist corrective (inherent in *any* form of communism) to the environmentalists who now make a fetish of nature in order to escape hard political and economic facts. What communism – and the Christian gospel no less clearly – are saying to the industrialized nations is that, 'if there is not a drastic redistribution of wealth both on a global scale and within nations, coupled to a drastic overhaul of political institutions, the species *homo sapiens* faces extinction'.[5]

It is essential that the best minds should go on debating the limits of growth and that governments should – however tentatively – plan to act on these insights. But for the next few decades it appears as good as certain that there will be no general scientific consensus. The debate on the sources and potential sources of energy has obviously only just begun. And the passionate debate on the population explosion will also go on raging. It should not have taken the Bucharest world conference to demonstrate that Western prophets of population doom will not be taken seriously as they try to stop others from 'breeding irresponsibly', instead of conceding that population-growth – already at zero level in much of the Western world and in Eastern Europe – is at present the product of exploitation, illiteracy and poverty. Economic injustice is the fundamental problem.

Without economic justice a call for population-control and a limitation of capital growth in the poor world is unrealistic and lacks credibility. Experience has already shown this to be true. Birth-control campaigns in India and Brazil simply will not work. But given planned investment and the conditions necessary for social disciplines to operate, i.e. *basically* decent standards of living (as in China), population-growth naturally levels out. These are insights being learnt by experience which Marxists have long accepted. Capitalism in the form of neo-imperialism has tried to avoid these conclusions because they point to the need for socialism within nations and between nations.

As long as profit for individuals, corporate bodies or even whole powerful nations remains the driving force of economic planning, the imbalance between man and his environment is bound to continue. The Marxist concept of alienation is highly complex and not wholly understood by most Marxists themselves – but reduced to its simplest terms it is proving to be absolutely true: when men are exploited for profit, they have no organic relationship to the product of their work. Their creativity is taken from them and the result is the disintegration of personal and social harmony. In addition, exploitation – as we now see – while dehumanizing the exploiter and the exploited also destroys man's natural environment and alienates him from nature. Technology, serving the profit motive, becomes master over man, and the parable of the sorcerer's apprentice becomes true: the magic machine man has created to do his work takes over and destroys both the environment and, in the end, man himself.

None of this is to say that communists have found the right practical answers. The state monolith controlling all the means of production and distribution is not necessarily socialism, and Eastern Europe demonstrates that changes in property relationship do not, of themselves, solve either moral or technical problems. The material and spiritual needs of man cannot be ideologically imposed, however 'correct' the ideology. Private enterprise, leading to monopoly capitalism, has so far been hell-bent on trying to dictate both to men and nature that all activity promoting capital growth is, in the end, beneficial. It is a lie, now exposing itself. Capitalism, simply taken over by bureaucracy, does not solve any of the problems. But, as the Chinese experiment might suggest, it is just possible that the devolution of power on the commune pattern, with local people *in touch with nature* (with material and educational resources fairly shared), can lead to genuinely organic development of both land and the product of men's creativity in intermediate and controlled higher technology. Then, when men are no longer hungry and begin to produce in ways that are consonant with their environment, they are given spiritual as well as material satisfaction. When that happens, even the potentially dangerous population explosion ceases to be a threat and becomes subject to freely accepted social disciplines.

In conclusion, a Marxist understanding of man, work and nature does not of itself solve technical problems. It does, however, provide at least a partially valid theoretical base for the actions which men must take to change the world for the better. It is a basis in which an increasing number of people – many of them Christians – place considerable trust. That is specially true in Asia and Latin America. It is much less true in Russia and Eastern Europe where communist ideology has largely gone sour. No amount of lip-service can hide the disillusionment.

At this point a short personal critique, largely arising out of dialogue between Christians and Marxists in recent years, may perhaps be permitted. Marxist insights seem most defective where they fail to allow a degree of real dignity to the natural order and assume that man is limitlessly powerful and therefore ultimately in a position to build paradise *solely in his own interest*. Christians have tended to make a comparable mistake. Many theologians in the Judeo-Christian tradition see both the Creation and the Incarnation as stemming from God, proceeding to man and going back to God, with all the rest of the natural order as simply a scenario for this process instead of an area with its own distinctive holiness. When that holiness is ignored and man's creative labour is unrelated to it, then the harmony of the whole natural order is broken. Wholeness, holiness, health are undermined. Conflict between man and nature ensues, man banishes himself to somewhere 'east of Eden', and through this process of alienation the inherent unity of the created order is destroyed.

It is far too early to affirm, but it is just conceivable that, in the context of the ancient culture and philosophy of China, informed by Marxist insights with their Jewish, Christian and humanist roots, man may be beginning to save creation from himself, may really have begun to build communism and may be setting out on the long road to a new wholeness. Christians might usefully ask themselves what relation this might have – personally and socially – to what Jesus calls the Kingdom.

But I have no wish to end in a starry-eyed way. The efforts of human beings everywhere will be needed to solve immense technical problems. MIT's research into the limits of growth will need to be taken as seriously as the lessons of the Chinese communes. Inspiration will be needed, and ethical criteria. Marxism at its best can provide both. But distorted into a rigid dogma it can kill imagination and destroy moral judgement. That is also true of Christianity. Positively, Marxism rightly affirms that no longer will the rich be able to dictate to the poor who shall inherit the earth and when. The implementation of economic justice remains a prerequisite for righting the imbalance between man, the product of his labour and the world in which he lives. To affirm that this is possible is a hopeful and still a revolutionary idea.

GOD AND THE FUTURES
OF MAN

by Don Cupitt

Belief and Atheism

In the report it has been argued that the recovery of belief in
God the Creator is the key to mankind's future well-being. It
will not be quite the same belief as before, for we know now
that nature, as well as man, has a history; and this makes it
impossible to represent God's relation to the world as Milton,
for example, portrayed it. We have to think of man, not as
inserted into a world ready-made for him, but as slowly
evolving within and differentiating himself out of the world-
process. Man continuously adapts himself to the world, and
the world to himself. Belief in God binds together the self and
the world; the history and destiny of man, and the history and
destiny of man's environment. God's sovereign spirituality, his
absolute knowledge of the world, his intimate presence to it,
and his self-effacing government of it, are the ideals towards
which, over millions of years, the human spirit haltingly moves.
Man's self-awareness, knowledge and action are kept from
scepticism, despair and destructiveness in so far as he can think
of himself and the world as joint and interdependent products of a single creative purpose, moving towards a blessed
destiny.

But the claim that God is central to the future of man may
still seem very strange at this time of day. For surely its atheism
is an essential feature of the modern world-view? The world

that came to birth in theory between Copernicus and Newton, and in practice in the industrial revolution, is one in which nature is precisely *not* any longer perceived as creation. The modern way of looking at nature depends upon empirical observation and mathematical analysis. The discernment in nature of objective value and the workings of a personal Providence were expressly excluded from the first. Belief in God retreated for a while (*c.* 1700–1860) within the self, but since Darwin that last citadel has fallen with the progressive extension of the scientific method to man himself. Just as the configuration of a flower came to be explained, not in terms of divine design, but in terms of its biological development and function; so religious beliefs in the individual, and religious institutions in society, came to be explained in terms of their psychological and sociological functions respectively. Whether as personal conviction or as social institution, belief in God could no longer be seen as more than a survival from the days when people did perceive the universe in personal categories. But nowadays our apprehension of the world has become very much more finely discriminating, and we simply cannot see a phenomenon like the weather as the expression of divine pleasure or displeasure. In an important sense, we are all atheists nowadays. Surely it must be concluded that if belief in God survives among educated people it does so as a gesture of loyalty to the past, or as a morally and artistically attractive fiction which must be believed to be more than a fiction in order to work *as* a fiction, but *not* as a way of actually cognizing the world's meaning?

So, if we say that belief in God must return, we need to explain why there has had to be so long and substantial an atheistic phase in the development of mankind. If modern atheism is not a permanent achievement, but a temporary phase, what is its theological meaning? And what will a future world in which men again believe in God be like?

Here we differ again from men of earlier periods, in that our collective awareness, and our knowledge of and power over nature, have become so highly developed that we can now envisage a whole series of possible futures, between which we are (at least in theory) free to choose.

In our century most imaginative writers, projecting existing social trends, have envisaged a totalitarian future. As technology (particularly the means of storing, retrieving and transmitting information) develops, it irresistibly increases the size of organizations and concentrates real power in fewer hands. Over-population, and the consequent scarcities, seem to require that a very tight social discipline be imposed in the future to avert general disaster. During our century the state has continually grown in power in every country, by popular demand. So science-fiction writers have been dominated by an image of the society of the future which recalls Plato's *Republic*. There are some who welcome this prospect, like the psychologist B. F. Skinner, in his instructive novel *Walden Two*.[1] Others, influenced by the chapter called 'The Grand Inquisitor' in *The Brothers Karamazov*, say on the contrary that the barbarous old world, in which men were at least free, is to be preferred to the hedonistic planned Utopia men are now trying to build. Evgeny Zamyatin's *We*[2] and Aldous Huxley's *Brave New World*[3] belong here. Even H. G. Wells, in 'A Story of the Days to Come',[4] is uneasy about what lies ahead; but it needed electronic communications, and the horrors of twentieth-century German and Russian experience, to create George Orwell's *1984*.[5] But whether the future be seen in the image of a well-planned holiday camp, or in that of Stalinism, collectivism remains the prospect; and perhaps it will come, if we go on choosing comfort rather than freedom, Caesar rather than Christ.

For the first choice is, as it has always been, that between Caesar and Christ. Most people in our culture believe there is another possibility. Something called 'liberalism', 'humanism', or 'Western values' is held up as an alternative to totalitarianism. It is a broken reed. It is shot through with technological rationality and utilitarian ethics, so that it not merely offers no resistance to totalitarianism; it actively facilitates its development. The dominant outlook in the West is sceptical in metaphysics and religion, sceptical or at *best* utilitarian in ethics, empiricist in its theory of knowledge, and puts its trust in the empirical sciences and them alone. It has no power to oppose totalitarianism. In fact, if we look for historical precedents for this temper of mind, we find them among the privileged classes of a civilization in decline, during the lethargic Indian summer before their destruction. Like well-to-do pagans in late antiquity, or like the characters in Chekhov's plays, such people are too effete and worldly-wise to be able to understand or wield the great religious forces which create civilizations.[6] While such an outlook remains dominant, the Marxists (God help us) are right: nothing can stop the promised movement towards the totalitarianism which (despite their protestations) they in fact promote.

But there are other possibilities, though not all of *them* are good either. There are at least three possible futures for religious belief. We can call them stories, and write them out as follows.

Possible Futures

The first story runs like this: a modern industrial state needs abundant energy and a steady supply of some fifteen or so basic raw materials to survive. But few of the leading powers have adequate indigenous supplies of more than about half of them. We are now entering a time of acute shortages, economic stress and national rivalries. After having been checked for a decade, the proliferation of nuclear weapons is beginning again. So we are entering an age when a great power can quickly be brought to the pitch of desperation at which it seriously contemplates the use of nuclear weapons. In fact over the next fifty years or so a major thermonuclear war in the northern hemisphere is likely. It will make much of the planet uninhabitable, and severely damage the entire biosphere. The remnant of the human race will need to create a strictly disciplined society which ruthlessly eliminates the genetically damaged among its offspring. God will be seen as lawgiver and judge; an avenging Father who has terribly punished man's overweening pride and folly. Men must henceforth bow to the yoke of a harsh religious law, and eke out a kind of frontier life in the relatively unpolluted southern hemisphere.

This is roughly the plot of John Wyndham's *The Chrysalids*,[7] and it is undeniably one form a future revival of belief in God might take. It *is* a future men may choose. We may hope they will not, and be sure they ought not to, but who can be certain that it will not happen? It would be *one* outcome of the conflict between religious and scientific ways of looking at the world; but a reactionary outcome, involving a rejection of modern science and a reversion to an older world-picture. It is perhaps improbable, for nowadays the literature, the personnel, the equipment and the institutions of modern science extend to all corners of the earth. Even if there were only a million survivors, and they in the southernmost inhabited lands, the bulk of modern scientific knowledge and skills would survive. And in a post-holocaust world it would be highly useful. However bad their state of shock, it is hard to see the survivors of a holocaust wilfully destroying something so obviously valuable.

The second story is this: that 'scientific rationality', the entire set of mind and body of assumptions which comprise the scientific habit of mind and motivate the scientific community – the entire faith in the progress of knowledge along *these* particular lines – may crumble internally. Some say this is already happening, and point to the long tradition of literary hostility (to name a few names: Blake, Kierkegaard, Nietzsche, John Cowper Powys, Lawrence, and Roszak), public scepticism about the benefits of technology, and relativism among the theorists. The intake of new recruits through the universities may decline further. Men may switch from mass-production to handicrafts; from high-technology agriculture and processed foods to home-grown vegetables; from mass-communications, mechanized transport and large organizations to local fellowship, Shanks's pony and low-energy living; from nationalism and modern weaponry to non-violence and world citizenship.

If shifts of this kind took place on a very large scale – and, after all, many of them are highly desirable and many of them may become economic necessities – the cultural importance of the more costly kinds of science and technology would decline sharply. It is very expensive to produce a Ph.D. in physics, and still more so to keep him employed thereafter in a government-financed laboratory. It is easy to forget how much the development of science in the last sixty years has been spurred on by nationalism and militarism. In a less power-crazy world there might be less money spent on 'heavy' science, on such things as particle physics, and more on agricultural research and on the arts.

Would such a world be more religious? Yes it would – in a certain sense. We might find a great revival of the arts and crafts, of the inner life, and of every species of occultism and mysticism. What we would be less likely to see is any common and world-wide standards of rationality and community of world-view.

To many religious people such a world would be very attractive. It would be a gentler, more 'Aquarian' world, less dominated by 'masculine' aggression, impersonal power and analytical reason, and so giving more play to the 'feminine', intuitive and sensuous aspects of our natures. It might be a little like India at the peak of its civilization over a thousand years ago.

But it would not be a world friendly to belief in God. The writers who have been its prophets have been religious, but anti-theistic and irrationalist. To believe in God is to believe in one ultimate mind, and so in one ultimate standard of truth and goodness. The Aquarian world would lack intellectual unity; it would lack the ascetic drive to purge away error and confusion, and to move towards one objective final truth, which so profoundly links the modern scientific enterprise with belief in God. God and modern science are for ever squabbling and trying to undermine each other (and I have stressed their hostility), but their quarrels are those of a married couple, not of simple enemies. When they both realize what the Aquarian world entails they will forget their quarrel and join forces against it. Certainly no true believer in God can wish for the collapse of the extraordinary intellectual movement which began in the sixteenth century and has steadily gathered momentum ever since. With all its unhappy side-effects, including the near-strangulation of its spouse, it still remains modern man's only great achievement, and somehow from within it the pattern of human destiny must be unfolded.

So I prefer a third story, which looks forward to the re-emergence of faith in God within the developing scientific enterprise itself, and so seeks to include the rise and growth of the scientific community within its theology of history.

The Spirit of Man

The history of human consciousness has to be constructed from very imperfect evidence. There are such historical and archae-ological data as survive; there are the remaining preliterate tribal societies; there is an analogy of it in the developing mind of the child; and there is our gradually deepening understanding of the experience and behaviour of animals. In addition, the great religions preserve precious elements of the early stages in the development of human thought.

The most general characteristic of the history of conscious-ness that we can discern is that it has been a prolonged and infinitely laborious effort to clarify and discriminate. At first there are no clear distinctions or definitions at all. The ideas of God, the world, society and the self are inchoate and con-fused. Distinguishing these objects, setting bounds about them, beginning to analyse their structure and relate them to each other, was a very slow and painful process.

The individual, society, and the world were understood

correspondingly, and it is common nowadays to suggest that the structure of one is used as a metaphor for the structure of another. Structural analogies between language, the body, society and the world are still present even in modern culture.

Here is an everyday example, stolen from Mary Douglas[8] and embellished. A typical modest English house is made and used to express a symbolism of the body, of society and of the world. It can be sketched as follows:

The house is shaped like a human body. Children draw the front of a house like a face, with the front door as the mouth, the front windows as eyes, and the roof as hair or a hat. (Note here the significant use of 'faceless' as a term of reproach in connection with architecture in the International Modern style.) At the back of the house, in its bowels, are private areas reserved for cooking, washing and excretion. The two floors of the house represent darkness and rest above, light and activity below. The bedrooms are occupied, from front to back, in order of status, and regularly diminish in size. Many people will remember how such important social events as courting and funeral teas took place in the front parlour.

Cleaning and tidying the house link categorizing the cosmos (a place for everything and everything in its place) with grooming the body. Its relation to the garden represents the relation of culture to nature. The proprieties of good and bad manners, clean and unclean habits, within the house express an ordering of life and of the world.

8. It is because the biologica
superseded by this psycho-soci
interplay of the Darwinian co
and mutation with man's consc
environment, and what he mak
the next stage of development as
of man himself – or his values
expression. But this is precisely w
that in and through Christ men
their true ends, those for which Go
that inner transformation which
life' in the Holy Spirit of God. In
our flesh (John 1:14), the Word t
Word may be to other intelligent
the future in the universe.

9. The approach outlined in this e
since in William Temple's *Nature, M*
he writes in somewhat Hegelian t
approach offered here provides a
Temple's penetrating insight into
sacraments for providing the basis o
of 'spirit'. The approach is also sim
Thornton, *The Incarnate Lord* (Longn
10. C. E. Raven, *Natural Religion an*
Lectures, vol. II (Cambridge Univers
p. 157.

11. Some might object that this view
should we suppose that man is the
Briefly, this is taken to be the case becau
man is now psycho-socially effective in
effects on other species; and, (2) theolo
was made flesh' of a *man*.

The Theology of Nature in the Eastern
Theologians
1. Eloi Leclerc, *Le Cantique des Creatures*,

There are still some people who think such structural
analogies far-fetched, so let me reinforce this one by recalling
how until very recently most people were firmly convinced
that there was a right shape for a church or a chair to be, and
that 'right shape' was anthropomorphic. The cruciform church
represents in detail the body of Christ on the cross, and the
names of the parts of a chair are the names of parts of the body:
back and seat, arms and legs.

Now in our large-scale and pluralistic society no single
symbolic structuring of experience is universally agreed and
enforced. Nobody will be seriously worried if the kitchen is
put at the front of the house. But in the past, through countless
ages, every aspect of life, all institutions, artefacts and relations,
were symbolically structured in order to express and to teach
the commonly held world-picture. Ideas about the self, about
society, about the world, and about the gods, all began, not so
much as mental constructions, but rather as patterns of symbolism built into social structures. Ideas about the self, about
society and about the world were clarified by means of rules
governing social life.

Ancient Israel and Greece made major advances. Israel's
great achievement was to sharpen the distinctions between God,
the elect people and the individual. God transcended the world:
no mundane symbolism could adequately represent him, no
ritual could guarantee his favour. Society's authority over the
individual was not absolute: the individual *contra mundum*
might after all be in the right. In the Old Testament perspective, for all its internal diversity, one thing is clear: that God,
the world, society and the self are more clearly distinguished
from each other than had ever been achieved before.

Add to this that the Greeks developed the idea of a relatively
autonomous natural order, that they largely discovered the

2. Death as a punishme[...]
of life, Genesis 25:8; 35[...]

On the Alleged Incompati[...]
1. *The Structure of Scie*[...]
Press, Chicago and Lond[...]
2. *Chance and Necessity*, [...]
3. ibid., pp. 164–5.
4. For example, A. Har[...]
1965, and World Publishi[...]
153ff.
5. *A Rumour of Angels* (D[...]
Lane, The Penguin Press, [...]

A Sacramental View of Natu[...]
1. This essay is an abridg[...]
Peacocke's article in *Thinki*[...]
(SCM Press, London, 1972).[...]
2. William Temple, *Readi*[...]
London, 1939), pp. xx–xxi.
3. ibid., p. xx.
4. Technically, these have [...]
constitutes the appropriate s[...]
'form' and intention – but in[...]
to physical reality at various[...]
notoriously ambiguous, and it[...]
what it is being contrasted.)
5. cf. William Temple, *Nature*[...]
1934; reprinted Macmillan, L[...]
York, 1964), ch. IV.
6. cf. O. C. Quick, *The Ch*[...]
1927).
7. A fuller account for the gener[...]
Science and the Christian Expe[...]
London and New York, 1971[...]
adopted here.

2[...]

There are still some people who think such structural analogies far-fetched, so let me reinforce this one by recalling how until very recently most people were firmly convinced that there was a right shape for a church or a chair to be, and that 'right shape' was anthropomorphic. The cruciform church represents in detail the body of Christ on the cross, and the names of the parts of a chair are the names of parts of the body: back and seat, arms and legs.

Now in our large-scale and pluralistic society no single symbolic structuring of experience is universally agreed and enforced. Nobody will be seriously worried if the kitchen is put at the front of the house. But in the past, through countless ages, every aspect of life, all institutions, artefacts and relations, were symbolically structured in order to express and to teach the commonly held world-picture. Ideas about the self, about society, about the world, and about the gods, all began, not so much as mental constructions, but rather as patterns of symbolism built into social structures. Ideas about the self, about society and about the world were clarified by means of rules governing social life.

Ancient Israel and Greece made major advances. Israel's great achievement was to sharpen the distinctions between God, the elect people and the individual. God transcended the world: no mundane symbolism could adequately represent him, no ritual could guarantee his favour. Society's authority over the individual was not absolute: the individual *contra mundum* might after all be in the right. In the Old Testament perspective, for all its internal diversity, one thing is clear: that God, the world, society and the self are more clearly distinguished from each other than had ever been achieved before.

Add to this that the Greeks developed the idea of a relatively autonomous natural order, that they largely discovered the *a priori* realm, and that they enormously advanced the concept of classification; and the way was open for the abandonment of the old semi-conscious social and symbolic cosmologies. A universal spiritual Creator-God altogether transcended the old sacral-social world-pictures. Christianity rebelled against and declared redundant the old categorizing of reality in terms of sacred and profane, clean and unclean (for example, Mark 7:1–23; Acts 10:1–16). Human spirituality was ready to advance to a higher level of consciousness of itself under God, and a new relation to the world.

In practice, however, the process has proved as slow in Christian Europe as it had been in the pre-Christian Middle East. Once again one is reminded of how painful a labour, with how many setbacks, it has been to develop a more dif-ferentiated world-picture, and a more free and autonomous awareness of the self as spirit.

We have begun a fresh attempt in modern times, and from below. The Renaissance and the Reformation developed and liberated individual self-awareness, preparing the way for a new relation of the self to the world. As the ancients first derived their ideas of number and of the structure of time from the heavens, so we too began with astronomy, with dynamics and with mathematics. Like the old Ionians, we began with an absurd over-simplification, trying to give a complete account of the universe in terms of matter, motion and number.

Atheism and After

Inevitably these first modern cosmologies were mechanistic and implicitly atheistic, and seemed bleakly impersonal. It was very hard to see any relation between the self which had educed these cosmologies, and the world described in them – a difficulty still very acute in the time of Kant, and which he attempted to solve in the critical philosophy. Indeed, the alienation between thought and being, evidenced as early as Descartes and Pascal, is still a very marked feature of modern French culture; in the younger Sartre, for example, and in Jacques Monod.

So, in the seventeenth century, God, the world and the self were drastically distinguished from each other. In the process there were gains and losses. Among the losses, the decline of the arts and religion began, mind-body dualism became entrenched, and as the mechanistic cosmology began to work back into and reshape social relations, political, economic and social behaviour acquired an impersonal quantitative character. The form the industrial revolution took created a new class of people, the factory workers – a class religiously, culturally and economically deprived, and burning with a vast sense of injustice, the victims and the bearers of atheism.

But gradually, as more sciences developed, the world-picture became more complex. Upon the physics-and-mathematics base were erected further layers: chemistry, geology, biology, sociology, anthropology, psychology. New fundamental concepts were added, and the effect has been gradually to close the gap between thought and being. The alienation between the mind and the world is becoming gradually less acute. We can now begin to think about the relation between the structure of thinking and the various world-structures as represented in thought. We can, that is, begin to set side by side man's developing self-awareness and his successive cosmologies, and look to some kind of convergence. We can dimly see the relation of the absolute Creator-Spirit to the world as it is as the ideal to which, through all these millennia, the human mind has been striving. The succession of worlds which the human mind has made, arranged in a series of slowly growing clarity and complexity, points to the world as it truly is in the absolute mind of God.

In the twentieth century the world-picture of modern science has at last spread all over the world, and so begun to create the first-ever common cosmology for the entire human race. It continues to evolve, both through occasional theoretical revolution, and through its continually increasing internal differentiation. As it becomes richer, more many-levelled and more powerful, we see that it begins to reincorporate previously expelled ethical and personal categories; giving promise, let us hope, of a more humane future. But it must not lose its original intellectual rigour. The problem is to combine the process of enrichment with the maintenance of common standards of rationality, so as to prevent it breaking up into a variety of disparate languages.

So the emergence of an immensely rich and detailed cosmology of the world as creation can perhaps be dimly envisaged as taking place over the next century or so, bringing with it a more genuinely humane and unified culture. It will be world-wide, and will require at least as large a development of the human spirit again as has taken place over the last three centuries. Trace, for example, the idea of the chimpanzee through Edward Tyson,[9] G. L. L. Buffon,[10] T. H. Huxley and Jane Goodall. Man's understanding of himself in this period has enlarged by as much as his understanding of the chimpanzee. (Indeed, it's amusing that animals are still, as much as in the remotest prehistory, a mirror to us. Soon after Chomsky's *Syntactic Structures*[11] appeared in 1957 some zealous Americans began to teach a sign-language to chimpanzees and to demonstrate that they too have the rudiments of syntax.)

What we are looking for, then, is nothing less than a gradual convergence of the spirit of science and the spirit of religion, a reconciliation of analytical and intuitive reason. I want nothing of Teilhard de Chardin's mystical collectivism, nor of his belief in inevitable progress, but I do say that it is possible to overcome the deep antinomies in our present culture. Indeed, since social structures lag behind scientific developments, we can see that much that is wrong in our society is so because it is anachronistic in terms of knowledge we already have. The intercontinental airline pilot's way of life and work-schedules are biologically wrong and damaging in terms of knowledge we already have about the human body's physiological rhythms. The design of a motor assembly line is manifestly wrong in terms of what we know already about the human being as worker. Intensive agriculture, with its predominantly engineering-and-chemistry approach, is questionable in terms of biological knowledge we already have. The bleak functionalism of the concrete jungle is anachronistic in terms of what we already know about man's need for symbols, his need to live in symbiosis with animals and plants, and so on. The fact that the life sciences, and the sciences of man, only got under way centuries after the physical sciences is at the root of many of our present discontents, and we can already see clearly many of the changes that need to be made.

From the eighteenth to the mid-twentieth centuries public life was on the whole dominated by an atheistic and mechanistic cosmology, which found expression in exploitative attitudes both to nature and to the industrial worker. In the same period religion, morality and art retreated more and more into a psychological realm to which few outside the *bourgeoisie* could gain access. Today, technological rationality and human spirituality are still far apart. We can see this, for example, in the absurd divisions, and the failure to make connections, between the arts pages and the financial pages in the newspaper. But there are some signs of convergence, a convergence which would transform our lives and the way we treat nature and our fellow-men. Its achievement would be the rebirth of faith in God, the relating of all aspects of our experience to One who is holy, all-wise and all-good.

NOTES

THE REPORT

1. Introduction: The world we live in
1. The UN Conference on Population at Bucharest in 1974 could agree neither on the nature of the problem nor on any solution. Unfortunately the Christian Churches were officially represented only by a Vatican delegation. For a non-Roman Catholic approach, see the World Council of Churches publication *Population Policy, Social Justice and the Quality of Life* (Geneva, 1973), and *Study Encounter*, vol. ix, no. 4 (1973).
2. Peter Mathias (ed.), *Science and Society, 1600–1900* (Cambridge University Press, London, 1972), p. 163.
3. J. Ernest Renan, *L'Avenir de la Science* (written 1848–9, pub. Paris, 1890).
4. See Ian T. Ramsey, *Words about God* (SCM Press, London, and Harper & Row, New York, 1971), pp. 202ff.
5. cf. H. Montefiore, *Doom or Deliverance?* (Manchester University Press, Manchester, 1972), p. 27.

2. The God who creates
1. *The Fearful Void* (Hodder & Stoughton, London, 1974), p. 38.
2. *The Mystery of Existence* (New York, 1965), pp. 178ff.
3. cf. Basil Mitchell, *The Justification of Religious Belief* (Macmillan, London, 1973, and Seabury Press, New York, 1974).
4. For a fuller discussion, see essay on 'Biblical Attitudes to Nature', pp. 87ff. below.
5. *The Edges of Language* (SCM Press, London, and Macmillan, New York, 1972), p. 83.
6. *Chance and Necessity* (Knopf, New York, 1971, and Collins, London, 1972).
7. Some theologians at present are giving fresh consideration to the idea of creation as the expression of the overflow of divine generosity.

This involves a reassessment of the gratuitousness and exuberance of God's action, cf. J. Moltmann, *Theology and Joy* (SCM Press, London, 1973), or Harvey Cox, *The Feast of Fools* (Harvard University Press, Cambridge, Mass., and London, 1969).

8. See essay 'On the Alleged Incompatibility between Christianity and Science', pp. 121ff. below.

9. F. Gogarten, *Verhängis und Hoffnung der Neuzeit* (Stuttgart, 1953).

10. Harvey Cox, *The Secular City* (SCM Press, London, and Macmillan, New York, 1965).

11. J. Metz, *Theology of the World*, trans. W. Glen-Doepel (Burns & Oates, London, and Herder & Herder, New York, 1969).

12. op. cit., pp. 24, 23.

13. *Science, Technology and Society in Seventeenth-Century England* (1938; reprinted Fertig, New York, 1970).

14. *One-dimensional Man* (Routledge & Kegan Paul, London, 1964).

15. *The Making of a Counter Culture* (Doubleday, New York, 1969, and Faber & Faber, London, 1970).

16. *The Divine Relativity* (Yale University Press, New Haven and London, 1948), and *Philosophers Speak of God* (University of Chicago Press, Chicago and London, 1953).

17. *Exploration into God* (SCM Press, London, 1967), p. 83.

18. *The Openness of Being* (Darton, Longman & Todd, London, 1971, and Westminster Press, Philadelphia, 1972), p. 162.

19. *The Go-Between God* (SCM Press, London, 1972), p. 26.

20. *Wesen des Christentums* (1841), trans. as *The Essence of Christianity* (1854; reprinted Harper & Brothers, New York and London, 1957), ch. XI.

21. *An Introduction to the Study of Man* (Clarendon Press, Oxford, 1971), pp. 640–1.

22. *The Ascent of Man* (BBC Publications, London, 1973), p. 412.

23. cf. H. Montefiore, *The Question Mark* (Collins, London, 1969), p. 53.

24. *Institutes*, book II, ch. I.5.

25. For further discussion of 'natural evil', see essay below, pp. 110ff.

3. The scope of salvation

1. Doubleday, New York, 1970, and Allen Lane, The Penguin Press, London, 1972.

2. *Essays on Nature and Grace* (Fortress Press, Philadelphia, 1972).

3. Westminster Press, Philadelphia, 1972. *The Freedom of Man Paul Verghese*

4. op. cit., p. 55.

5. ibid., p. 59.

6. cf. Christopher Derrick, *The Delicate Creation* (Tom Stacey, London, 1972), p. 99.

7. A fuller treatment of this theme will be found in the essay on 'The Theology of Nature in the Eastern Fathers and among Anglican Theologians', pp. 143ff. below.

8. *The Laws of Ecclesiastical Polity* (1899), I.2.V.

9. cf. pp. 46f., 57, 59f., and essay on 'A Sacramental View of Nature', pp. 132ff. below.

10. George Every, *Basic Liturgy* (Faith Press, London, 1961), p. 7. This book contains examples of such prayers.

11. For further discussion, see essay on 'A Sacramental View of Nature', pp. 132ff. below.

12. SCM Press, London, 1973. *46*

13. op. cit., p. 44.

14. See essay 'On "The Historical Roots of Our Ecological Crisis"', pp. 155ff. below.

15. See essay on 'The Theology of Nature in the Eastern Fathers and among Anglican Theologians', pp. 143ff. below.

16. Eloi Leclerc, *Le Cantique des Creatures, ou les Symboles de l'Union* (Paris, 1971), p. 28.

17. *Les Plus Vieux Textes du Carmel*, ed François de Ste Marie, OCD (Paris, 1944), p. 183.

18. cf. Barbara Ward and René Dubos, *Only One Earth* (André Deutsch, London, and Norton, New York, 1972), p. 144.

19. See W. Lowrie, *Kierkegaard*, vol. II (Harper, New York, 1962), pp. 540f.

20. cf. *The Ascent of Mount Carmel.*

21. David Jenkins in the introduction to J. Moltmann's *Theology and Joy*, p. vi.

22. See essay 'On the Alleged Incompatibility between Christianity and Science', pp. 121ff. below.

23. From the ordination service in the Byzantine rite.

24. *The New Consciousness in Science and Religion*, pp. 117–18.

25. See the chapter 'On the Holy Spirit' in *Ultimate Questions, An Anthology of Modern Russian Religious Thought*, ed. Alexander Schmemann (Holt, Rinehart & Winston, New York, 1965).

26. *The Agreed Statement on the Eucharist* of the International Anglican-Roman Catholic Commission.

27. cf. p. 39 above.

28. See essay on 'A Sacramental View of Nature', pp. 132ff. below.

4. From theology to ethics

1. See essay on 'Biblical Attitudes to Nature', pp. 87ff. below.

2. See essay on 'Some Evidence from Other Religions', pp. 159ff. below.

3. See essay on 'Marxism, Nature and Work', pp. 169ff. below.

4. R. L. Shinn, *Man: The New Humanism* (Lutterworth Press, London, and Westminster Press, Philadelphia, 1968), pp. 170ff.

5. See *Alienation*, ed. F. Johnson (Academic Press, New York, 1973), for a comprehensive study of the many forms of alienation and of how they are connected.

6. e.g. *Changing Directions, the Report of the Independent Commission on Transport* (Coronet Books, London, 1974).

7. See essay on 'God and the Futures of Man', pp. 180ff. below.

THE ESSAYS

Biblical Attitudes to Nature

1. In addition to its use to refer to individual countries, the Hebrew word *'ereṣ*, 'earth', also denotes the whole terrestrial land-mass. There is, however, no clear instance of its being used, as we use it, as a name for land and sea combined, and it certainly never includes the heavens.

2. 'She shall be called *'iššā*, for she was taken out of *'īš*.' As is well known, St Jerome, in an attempt to convey the Hebrew pun, which

NOTES

comes through in English better than in most languages, rendered:
'She shall be called *virago*, for she was taken out of *vir*.' (!)
3. The view put forward in John Black, *The Dominion of Man*
(Edinburgh University Press, Edinburgh, 1970), pp. 40f., that there
is a conflict on this point between the two creation stories is therefore not tenable. It is simply not true to say that 'nowhere in the
Jahwist narrative . . . is man given dominion over the animals' (p.
41). But other points made by Professor Black are sensitive and
illuminating.
4. In fact both 'created' and 'made' (Genesis 1:26,27). As is well
known, the verb *bārā'*, 'create', is found in the Old Testament only
with God as subject. The significance of this is hard to assess. Because the Old Testament is, to all intents and purposes, the only
Hebrew literature of its period that we possess, we have no means
of knowing whether *bārā'* had a secular use, and if so, what that was.
Etymologically, it has so far been linked only with an ancient South
Arabian verb meaning 'to build', and a verb in the dialect of Socotra
meaning 'to bear, bring forth'. If it was capable of more abstract
connotations than the verb *'āsā*, 'make', which is the normal Hebrew
word for all making activities (just as the words 'build' and 'con-
struct' can bear more extended, metaphorical meanings in English),
then it may be that 'orthodox' writers adopted it in order to minimize the naïve pictorialism of such stories as Genesis 2:4bff.; but
we can only conjecture. It is found in the Old Testament only in the
Priestly writer, Deuteronomy, Jeremiah, Second and Third Isaiah,
Amos, Psalms, Malachi, and Ecclesiastes. With the possible but
unproven qualification already mentioned, there is no reason to
think that there is any substantial difference of meaning in the ultimate analysis between 'create' and 'make'; the collocation of the
two words at the end of the Priestly creation story (Genesis 2:3) is,
as it naturally seems, a sonorous full close for stylistic effect, not a
deliberate covering of two distinct theological concepts. Certainly
there are no grounds for reading into *bārā'* anywhere in the Old
Testament the content of later metaphysical understandings of the
idea of creation, such as *creatio ex nihilo*, which is not found in
Jewish religious writing until 2 Maccabees 7:28.

5. The same promise, though not in a covenant form, occurs as the climax of the older strand in the Flood story (Genesis 8:21-2).

6. We need to remember that the Old Testament primal myths differ from those of other ancient Near Eastern peoples in one very important respect. In other cultures the myths are played out in a 'timeless' world, which has no direct link with the present. This enables them to be used annually in a quasi-magical fashion at cultic festivals, because what they really express is the endlessly repeated patterns underlying natural cycles – death and rebirth, cosmos and chaos, light and darkness, conflict and victory, and so on. The Hebrew creation stories, on the other hand, are firmly characterized by the Old Testament as once-for-all parts of the historical process. This is done by the simple, and therefore often overlooked device of the genealogy. 'When Adam had lived a hundred and thirty years, he became the father of . . . Seth' (Genesis 5:3) may be most people's idea of an Old Testament passage completely devoid of religious value. In fact it is one of the most significant verses in the Old Testament, precisely because it welds the primal pair firmly into a chain of descent which, in theory at any rate, could be traced down to every living Israelite. The creation narrative is meant not as the symbolic expression of a theological truth about all existence but as an account of the beginning of history and the causes of later developments.

7. Only slaughter for food is explicitly mentioned here. The older creation story has God clothe Adam and Eve, on their expulsion from the garden, in skins, without stopping to explain how these are obtained (Genesis 3:21) – an oversight which, like the unaccountable existence of Cain's wife, is quite characteristic of unsophisticated stories. But presumably the divine decree in Genesis 9:2 is taken common-sensically to sanction the provision of all human needs by animal slaughter. Whether so-called 'sport' would have been considered a legitimate need is another question.

8. cf., for example, Psalms 19:1-6; 65:9-13; 84:3; 136; 148.

9. Job, Proverbs, Ecclesiastes, in the Old Testament proper; Wisdom of Solomon and Ecclesiasticus, in the Apocrypha.

10. And indeed, more than 'fair', since one of the marks of righteous-

ness or justice in the Old Testament is not a mere even-handedness but active favour to the defenceless and deprived.

11. By a process not uncommon in the Old Testament, and known as 'historicization', his destruction appears to be linked with the children of Israel's crossing of the Red Sea on their Exodus from Egypt. A similar association of the killing of the great sea-monster with the Exodus occurs in Isaiah 51:9–10, but here the monster's name is 'Rahab', a mocking name in the Isaiah tradition for Egypt: cf. Isaiah 30:7.

12. This point is also well made by John Black, op. cit., pp. 39f.: 'Although the theology of this book has been described as "strange" and "difficult", it is one which might, if properly examined, be found to have a peculiar appeal to the so-called "post-Christian" age of the twentieth century, both in the type of problem dealt with and the solutions put forward.'

13. The criticism of much present-day Christian preaching, for example, as being still too much concerned with these two things only, instead of having something to say on corporate and global issues, tends to ignore the fact that in the foundation (and still authoritative) documents of the Church precisely these were the overwhelmingly dominant concerns. Christianity was from the start a religion of individual faith and morals, its corporate consciousness related not to membership of mankind but to membership of the elect community drawn out from mankind by its response to the Gospel. The question whether anything specifically Christian, yet of wider import, can develop from this basic character is one with which the Church today is intensely exercised, and this report is one more small symptom of that concern.

14. Quotations from R. Bultmann, *Primitive Christianity* (Thames & Hudson, London, 1956), 'Hellenism', ch. II.

Natural Evil

1. William King, *De Origine Mali* (Dublin and London, 1702), ch. II, para. II; G. W. Leibniz, *Essais de Theodicée* (1710), 1.21 (trans. E. M. Huggard as *Theodicy* (Routledge & Kegan Paul, London, 1951), p. 136).

2. Death as a punishment, Genesis 2:17; 3:19; and as the fulfilment of life, Genesis 25:8; 35:29; 49:29–33.

On the Alleged Incompatibility between Christianity and Science
1. *The Structure of Scientific Revolutions* (University of Chicago Press, Chicago and London, 1962).
2. *Chance and Necessity*, p. 164.
3. ibid., pp. 164–5.
4. For example, A. Hardy, *The Living Stream* (Collins, London, 1965, and World Publishing, Cleveland and New York, 1968), pp. 153ff.
5. *A Rumour of Angels* (Doubleday, New York, 1969, and Allen Lane, The Penguin Press, London, 1970).

A Sacramental View of Nature
1. This essay is an abridged and slightly revised version of Dr Peacocke's article in *Thinking about the Eucharist*, ed. I. T. Ramsey (SCM Press, London, 1972).
2. William Temple, *Readings in St John's Gospel* (Macmillan, London, 1939), pp. xx–xxi.
3. ibid., p. xx.
4. Technically, these have been denoted as the 'matter' which constitutes the appropriate sacrament in contrast to its particular 'form' and intention – but in the present discussion 'matter' refers to physical reality at various levels of complexity. (The word is notoriously ambiguous, and it is always important to be clear with what it is being contrasted.)
5. cf. William Temple, *Nature, Man and God* (Macmillan, London, 1934; reprinted Macmillan, London, and St Martin's Press, New York, 1964), ch. IV.
6. cf. O. C. Quick, *The Christian Sacraments* (Nisbet, London, 1927).
7. A fuller account for the general reader is given in A. R. Peacocke, *Science and the Christian Experiment* (Oxford University Press, London and New York, 1971), which elaborates the approach adopted here.

8. It is because the biological evolution of man has now been superseded by this psycho-social development, which involves an interplay of the Darwinian combination of heredity, environment and mutation with man's conscious choice of what he makes of his environment, and what he makes of himself, that one can only see the next stage of development as some kind of inner transformation of man himself – or his values and his ability to attain their true expression. But this is precisely what the Christian gospel is, namely, that in and through Christ men have the opportunity of attaining their true ends, those for which God made them, and of experiencing that inner transformation which constitutes the essence of 'eternal life' in the Holy Spirit of God. In Christ, God the Word was made *our* flesh (John 1:14), the Word to us as men, whatever form his Word may be to other intelligent beings who may exist now or in the future in the universe.

9. The approach outlined in this essay has been adumbrated long since in William Temple's *Nature, Man and God*, ch. XIX. But there he writes in somewhat Hegelian terms, and it is hoped that the approach offered here provides a contemporary elaboration of Temple's penetrating insight into the relevance of the Christian sacraments for providing the basis of a unified view of matter and of 'spirit'. The approach is also similar to that presented in L. S. Thornton, *The Incarnate Lord* (Longmans, London, 1928).

10. C. E. Raven, *Natural Religion and Christian Theology*, Gifford Lectures, vol. II (Cambridge University Press, Cambridge, 1953), p. 157.

11. Some might object that this view is too man-centred. Why should we suppose that man is the last stage of development? Briefly, this is taken to be the case because, (1) scientifically speaking, man is now psycho-socially effective in his own evolution and in his effects on other species; and, (2) theologically speaking, the 'Word was made flesh' of a *man*.

The Theology of Nature in the Eastern Fathers and among Anglican Theologians

1. Eloi Leclerc, *Le Cantique des Creatures*, pp. 197, 202.

2. V. Lossky, *The Mystical Theology of the Eastern Church* (James Clarke, London, 1957), pp. 110–11.

3. Gervase Mathew, *Byzantine Aesthetics* (John Murray, London, 1963), pp. 23–4.

4. F. J. A. Hort, *The Way, the Truth and the Life* (Macmillan, Cambridge and London, 1893), p. 213.

5. ibid., p. 180.

6. *The Laws of Ecclesiastical Polity*, III.11.8.

7. ibid., V.56.5.

8. *Summa Theologica*, I.VIII.3.

9. *The Laws of Ecclesiastical Polity*, II.2.1.

10. ibid., V.48.2.

11. H. R. McAdoo, *The Spirit of Anglicanism* (A. & C. Black, London, and Scribner's, New York, 1965), p. 312.

12. *Lux Mundi*, ed. C. Gore, 10th edn (John Murray, London, 1890), pp. 422–3.

13. A. M. Ramsey, *From Gore to Temple* (Longmans, London, 1960), p. 17. The first two chapters of this book are directly relevant to our theme.

On 'The Historical Roots of Our Ecological Crisis'

1. *Science*, vol. 155 (10 March 1967), pp. 1203–7.

2. So, for example, Max Nicholson, *The Environmental Revolution* (Hodder & Stoughton, London, and McGraw-Hill, New York, 1970), pp. 264ff.

3. J. Passmore has recently argued, in *Man's Responsibility for Nature* (Duckworth, London, and Scribner's, New York, 1974), that it was *Graeco*-Christian 'arrogance which generated a rapacious attitude to nature'. But this generalization also needs qualification since, although Stoicism (as Passmore argues) may have contributed to such an attitude, the Platonic tradition encouraged a gentler and more harmonious relationship of man with nature.

4. Appendix, p. 247, by T. H. White, following his translation and edition of a Latin bestiary of the twelfth century, published as *The Book of Beasts* (Jonathan Cape, London, 1954).

5. 'Biblical Attitudes to Nature', pp. 87ff. above; I. G. Barbour, in

Earth Might Be Fair, ed. I. G. Barbour (Prentice-Hall, Englewood Cliffs and Hemel Hempstead, 1972), chs. 1,9; T. Derr, *Ecology and Human Liberation*, a WSCF book, vol. III, no. 1 (1973, serial no. 7); J. Barr, 'Man and Nature – The Ecological Controversy and the Old Testament', in *Bulletin of the John Rylands Library*, 55 (1972).
6. For example, W. Eichrodt, *Theology of the Old Testament*, trans. J. A. Baker (SCM Press, London, 1967).
7. L. W. Moncrieff, 'The Cultural Basis of our Environmental Crisis', in *Science*, vol. 170 (30 October 1970), pp. 508–12, reprinted in *Western Man and Environmental Ethics*, ed. I. G. Barbour (Addison-Wesley, Reading, Mass., 1973), together with ref. 1 and a reply by L. White. See also Derr, op. cit., pp. 17ff.

Some Evidence from Other Religions
1. For a full account, see Kenneth Cragg's books about Islam: *The Dome and the Rock* (SPCK, London, 1964); *The Privilege of Man* (Athlone Press, London, 1968), esp. ch. 2; and *The Mind of the Quran* (Allen & Unwin, London, 1973).
2. Cambridge University Press, London, 1954.

Marxism, Nature and Work
1. *The Social Function of Science* (Routledge, London, 1939), pp. 415–16.
2. *Capital*, vol. 1, ch. 7, sect. 1.
3. ibid., vol. 2, ch. 15, sect. 10.
4. Richard Clarke, in *Marxism Today*, May 1974, p. 148.
5. John Mathews, in *Marxism Today*, July 1974, p. 220.

God and the Futures of Man
1. Macmillan, New York, 1948.
2. Written 1920; pub. in Eng. trans. Dutton, New York, 1959, and Jonathan Cape, London, 1970.
3. Chatto & Windus, London, 1932.
4. From *Tales of Space and Time* (Harper & Brothers, London and New York, 1899).
5. Secker & Warburg, London, 1949.

6. In John Passmore's able and learned *Man's Responsibility for Nature*, the author himself is discernibly troubled by a sense of the comical inadequacy of his own *Weltanschauung* to the problems ahead. And though he says he believes in 'Western civilization', he must realize that not one of its *makers* held views even *remotely* resembling his.

7. Michael Joseph, London, 1955.

8. *Natural Symbols*, 2nd edn (Barrie & Jenkins, London, 1973), p. 191.

9. *Anatomy of a Pygmie*, 1699.

10. See his *Correspondance* (Paris, 1860).

11. The Hague, 1957.

INDEX

Abel, 94
abortion, 80
accidie, 31
Acts of the Apostles, 106
Adam, 35, 162, 163, 200
affirmation, Christian, 50-2, 54-5. *See* renunciation
Africa, attitudes to environment in, 6, 159-61
agnosticism, 61
agriculture, 73, 185, 186; capitalist, 173; intensive, 193; North American, 6
Ahab, king of Israel, 93
ahimsa (non-violence), 69, 165-6, 167
alienation, 13, 76, 179; from God, 38, 65; interaction of all forms, 79-80, 198; Marxist concept, 177; between mind and world, 191
Amazon basin, 6
Amun-Re, 90
animals: degradation of relations between man and, 95-6; friendship with and compassion for, 49, 98, 146, 147, 200-1; Indian attitudes, 165-6; in Jesus' parables, 105; Marx on, 172; naming by Adam, 89; slaughter, 74, 81, 200
animism, refutation by objective science (Monod), 124-5
Anselm, St, 143
Anthony of Egypt, St, 52
anthropocentric illusion (Monod), 123
anthropocentrism, extreme, 12-13
apes, 12-13
asa (make), 18, 23, 199
asceticism, Indian, 165
Asia, 178
astral cults, 106
astrophysics, 135
atheism: modern, 180-1; and modern cosmologies, 190-1, 193
atoms, 136, 137, 140
Augustine, St, 39-40, 47, 143

baptism, vows of, 50, 53, 54, 76, 78
bara (create), 18, 199
Barth, Karl, 23
Behemoth, 97
belief in God: and 'Aquarian' world,

186-7; key to mankind's future well-being, 180-1; in a loving, 25, 27; reactionary renewal of, 184; rebirth of, 187, 194
Benedict, St, 157
Benthamism, 9
Berger, Peter, 131
Bernal, J. D., 170-1
bestiaries, medieval, 157, 204
biology: incompatibility with 'anthropocentric illusion', 123; molecular, 124, 135; and society, 193
biosphere, 184
birth-control, 176
birth-rate, 129
Black, John, 199, 201
Blake, William, 185
Bowker, John, 167
Boyle, Robert, 152
Brahma, 165
Brazil, 6, 176
Britain, 7, 9
Bronowski, J., 29
Brothers Karamazov, The, 147, 182
Brunner, Emil, 23
Buddhism, 38, 164, 165, 166-7
Buffon, G. L. L., 192
Buren, Paul van, 18

Cain, 94, 200
Calvin, J., 22, 23, 35; and exploitation of nature, 24
Cameroons, 160
capital punishment, 80-1
capitalism, 12, 119; and Calvinism, 24; and communism, 174-5; religion and rise of, 172
cattle, African tribal attitudes, 160, 161
Ceylon, 166
Ch'an Buddhism, 166
chance: and evolution, 19-20, 124-5, 128; and existence of universe, 18; and matter, 124-5, 127. *See also* Monod
chastity, 51, 52
Chekhov, A., 183
chimpanzee, 192
China: religious attitudes to nature, 166-7; and solution of present

INDEX

state, growth of power, 182
statistical laws, 127-8
stress, 74
structural analogies, 188-9
suffering, 36, 63
symbolism, 188-90

Taoism, 166, 167
Taylor, John V., 26
technology, 3, 4, 9-11, 73; in 'Aquarian'
world, 185; and capitalist production,
173; Chinese approach, 175, 178; and
concentration of power, 182; development, 156; differing views, 110-12;
ills resulting from Western, 75; and
the profit motive, 177; and solution
to mankind's problems, 75, 76
Teilhard de Chardin, P., 40-1, 144, 193
Temple, William, 132, 133, 154, 202,
203
Theoktistos, Fr, 147
theology: 'process', 25; and progress
of science and technology, 170;
relation of science to, 45-6, 122-3;
role in environmental crisis, 40,
77-82; 'of the secular', 23. See
creation, God
theology of nature, 14, 68, 106, 108,
143-5, 197; Anglican, 149-54;
Eastern, 145-9; and theology of
environment, 154; and theology of
sanctification of matter, 153-4
thermodynamics, second law of, 19, 20
thermonuclear war, 184
Thomas Aquinas, St, 151
Thornton, L. S., 154
Thunberg, Lars, 144
totalitarianism, 3; future, 182-3
Traherne, Thomas, 152
transcendent, 'rumours' of the, 131
transplants, 4
transport, 7, 73
Tyson, Edward, 192

United States of America, 3, 6
universe, 18, 19, 72; 'built up from
below', 115; and entropy, 20;
Franciscan vision, 145; man in, 134-7;

purpose of, 66; sacramental understanding of, 60. See world
utilitarianism, 8, 183

vegetarianism, 81, 94, 166
Verghese, Paul, 39, 47
vows, see baptism, monasticism

waste, 36, 63
wealth, 176
Weber, Max, 24
Wells, H. G., 182
Westcott, B. F., 41, 153
whales, 13
White, Lynn, 47, 48, 49; on
exploitative outlook, 155-8
Whitehead, A. N., 43
Wilson, Monica, 159
Wisdom, 26-7
Word: image of, 27; Incarnation of,
42, 203; man's response to, 45
Wordsworth, W., 48, 153
world: apocalyptic view, 106-7;
Christian view, 133-4; contingency,
16, 21; goodness of created, 41, 45,
47, 50, 67, 77, 105, 108; offering of
to God in Eastern liturgy, 148;
open-endedness, 57; relation to
Creator-Spirit, 191-2; renunciation
of, 50-5, 78; sacramental view, 42-3,
47-50, 59-60, 137-42; science and, 46,
122; secularization, 40; solidarity of
man with, 43-5, 48; and structural
analogies, 188-90; transcendent
interpretation, 131. See universe
world-view, need for religious, 13, 79-80
World War I, 3
World War II, 3, 9
Wyndham, John, 184

Yahweh, 100
Yangtze river, 161
Young, J. Z., 28-9
Yunnan, 161

Zambia, 161
Zamyatin, Evgeny, 182
Zen Buddhism, 166

213